THE ULTIMATE GUIDE TO
NON-FICTION
WRITING

The 'Whole School' Approach to Non-Fiction Writing

By Mathew Sullivan & Alan Peat

CREATIVE EDUCATIONAL PRESS LTD

PUBLISHED BY: Creative Educational Press Ltd
                       2 The Walled Garden
                       Grange Park Drive
                       Biddulph
                       Staffs
                       ST8 7TA

                       Tel: 07789938923
                       Fax: 01782 379398

PRINTED BY: York Publishing Services Ltd.,
                       64, Hallfield Road, Layerthorpe, York, YO31 7ZQ

DESIGN: Amy Doorbar

PROOFREADING: Tom Storey and David Bohill

Alan Peat   www.alanpeat.com
                      info@alanpeat.com

Mathew Sullivan   www.inspiredminds.eu
                      inspiredminds123@gmail.com

ISBN: 978-0-9932000-2-1

Also available from Creative Educational Press Ltd (www.thecepress.com):

Writing Exciting Sentences: Age 7 Plus *by Alan Peat*
A Second Book of Exciting Sentences *by Alan Peat and Mathew Sullivan*
50 Ways to Retell a Story: Cinderella *by Alan Peat, Julie Peat and Christopher Storey*
Get Your Head Around Punctuation (…and how to teach it!) *by Alan Peat*
The Elves and The Shoemaker 1897 *illustrated by John Harrold*
Writing Exciting Ghost Stories Age 9 Plus: Ghost Story Plot Skeletons *by Alan Peat*
(co-author Julie Barnfather)
Teaching Outstanding Persuasive Writing *by Alan Peat*
Developing Writing Through Comics *by Mathew Sullivan*
50+ iPad Lessons for Exciting Sentences *by Alan Peat and Lee Parkinson*
The Magic Stone *by Alan Peat (illustrated by John Harrold)*
Word Warriors *(CD-ROM Game) design by Simon Matthews*
Spelling Bee *(CD-ROM Game) design by Simon Matthews*

ALAN PEAT @alanpeat

Alan Peat is a Staffordshire based Independent Education Consultant with a national and international reputation for training which has an immediate, sustainable impact on literacy standards. Teachers from across the UK comment on how much children ENJOY writing as a result of Alan's techniques and approaches being used in the classroom.

His achievements have led to the award of a Fellowship of the Royal Society of Arts (F.R.S.A.) in 2003 and, most recently, a Fellowship of the Historical Association (F.H.A.) '...in recognition of a significant contribution to the promotion and knowledge of history.' (October 2010)

Alan's work is now being used in 22 countries.

Thanks:

To my wife Julie for all her editorial support and many contributing ideas. Tom Storey and David Bohill also deserve praise for their excellent proofreading and advice.

Thanks also to my mum and dad for their unwavering support and love.
Finally, many thanks to Mathew for his outstanding contributions, and his friendship.

MATHEW SULLIVAN @InspiredMind5

Mathew Sullivan is a class teacher and Literacy Co-ordinator at St. Richard's R.C. Primary School, Manchester. He provides CPD training for Alan Peat Ltd. on using comics to enhance literacy teaching. This has been evaluated as 'superb' and 'inspiring' by attendees. Mathew also works as a creative and pedagogic consultant for Manchester Metropolitan University's Comic SMART initiative. His techniques are implemented in secondary schools across Manchester.

Mathew has showcased his techniques and approaches in schools across the North West. His book, *Developing Writing Through Comics,* was published by Creative Educational Press Ltd in 2014 and he co-authored *A Second Book of Exciting Sentences* with Alan. Mat was graded 'outstanding' by Ofsted in 2013 and named Silk 106.9 Teacher of the Year in 2012. His first novel for children, *Melvin McGee: Zombie Hunter,* will be published later this year.

Thanks:

To the staff and pupils of St. Richard's for their inspiration.

Thanks to my family and friends for their support.

Thanks to Alan for the opportunity.

Thanks to my Nan for the best example of determination, hard work and spirit anyone could ever ask for.

Although *The Ultimate Guide to Non-Fiction* is intended to be a stand-alone publication, reference has been made to ideas first published in the following books:

Writing Exciting Sentences: Age 7 Plus by Alan Peat
A Second Book of Exciting Sentences by Alan Peat and Mathew Sullivan
Teaching Outstanding Persuasive Writing by Alan Peat
Get Your Head Around Punctuation (...and how to teach it!) by Alan Peat

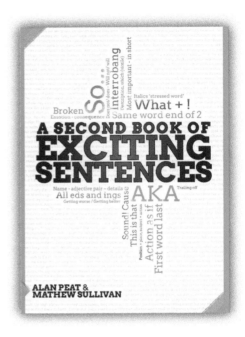

CONTENTS

INTRODUCTION

The first book I (Alan Peat) co-wrote on the subject of non-fiction writing was 'Improving Non-fiction Writing at Key Stages 1 & 2: The SUCCESS Approach' (Nash Pollock Publishing, 2004). In the decade which has passed since the publication of that book, I have delivered staff training, audited both reading and writing, and directly taught in many hundreds of schools ranging from urban to rural contexts; wealthy to underprivileged; multicultural (40+ languages) to monocultural etc. In all that time, and in all those varied contexts, three key factors have remained constant:

1. Pupils need to be overtly taught the structure/s of non-fiction text types.

2. Pupils need to be overtly taught the language features of non-fiction text types.

3. Pupils should both self-evaluate and peer review their writing with regard to the above two points **and** fitness for purpose (how well the writing matches/meets the needs of the intended audience).

These tenets were already established in 2004, and the term SUCCESS was employed as a helpful summative acronym -

S.   Structural
U.   Understanding +
C.   Confident
C.   Composition +
E.   Evaluation of
S.   Self =
S.   Successful Writing.

I still view these tenets as fundamentally important (though insufficient use was made of peer-reviewing opportunities, and significant advances in the Internet since 2004 have dramatically widened the potential range of audiences available to pupils). However, regular teaching of non-fiction over the last decade has demonstrated the need for two key improvements to the original book.

KEY IMPROVEMENT ONE: CAREFUL ANALYSIS OF THE PEDAGOGIC CONTEXT

The first essential step which schools must take on the path towards a sustainable approach to improving non-fiction writing is a careful analysis of the context/s in which non-fiction writing occurs.

A useful starting point would be a whole-staff discussion of the following six key pedagogic principles, which underpin the effective teaching of (and create a conducive environment for) dynamic, exciting non-fiction writing. The discussion should be framed by two questions:

1. What are we already doing in relation to the six key pedagogic principles?
2. What more could we do?

A well-structured, time-delineated action plan can then be developed based on staff responses.

The Six Key Pedagogic Principles

1. Engaging activities occur as precursors to writing.

All staff should be aware that the activities which directly precede the writing task will significantly affect (either positively or negatively) the writing itself. An interesting activity is far more likely to lead to interesting writing!

We recommend a broad range of experiential activities as effective stimuli for non-fiction writing. These include trips out: activities beyond the classroom (which could be as simple as a mini-beast hunt on a school playing field) as a stimulus for report writing. These kinds of stimuli can be thought of generically as 'going' activities: going to a museum, theatre, art gallery... or just going outside!

The second broad category of experiential stimulus may be termed 'making': making and testing paper aeroplanes; making a simple musical instrument; making a cake, etc. 'Making' activities are particularly likely to lead to more dynamic writing.

The third category of experiential stimuli is 'growing': growing plants; growing vegetables etc. The direct 'hands-on' aspect of this kind of activity makes it a powerful precursor to writing.

Staff should be encouraged to collectively discuss/brainstorm engaging activities which relate to each non-fiction genre. The categories suggested above are offered only as focal points for discussion. **Any** activity which engages the pupils should be regarded as valid.

2. Links are made with pupil interests.

Whenever possible, writing activities should be matched directly to pupil interests. For example, if pupils are writing persuasive texts, and the teacher knows that pupils A & B are interested in animals and pupils C & D love sport, then pupils A & B might productively write a persuasive essay on a theme like 'Why dogs are better pets than cats', whilst pupils C & D's theme might be 'Why football is better than netball'.

This form of interest-based differentiation is of vital importance - we all remember, engage with and work harder on that which interests us far more than that which bores us!

3. Talk comes 'first', 'during' and 'after'

Talk is (obviously) central to the raising writing standards agenda. If a pupil cannot **talk** about the structure and language features of a text type, then they certainly will not be able to **write** an effective example of the text type. Overt discussion of both the structural elements and the language features of non-fiction genres **must** occur prior to, during and after the writing process. Talk is not just a precursor to writing, it is a key analytical tool post-writing. Through structured talk, pupils learn to reflect upon and improve their initial drafts.

To assist with this process we have, throughout this volume, utilised a consistent-language approach to the structural elements of the text types. Many readers will be familiar with this approach as used in the books both Mathew Sullivan and I have written on the subject of sentence structure and development. The same principle - that **all** staff utilise **identical** vocabulary for the structural features of each text type - underpins this publication.

4. Links are made with material being read in class.

Many schools have a firmly established 'talk-into-writing' agenda, but often the equally important 'reading-into-writing' agenda is less securely embedded. We strongly advise that if a pupil is writing a specific text type, then, at the same time, they should be reading examples of that genre.

If this does not occur, then transfer of concepts from reading into writing will be reduced because of the time-gap. This is a matter which needs careful consideration (and budget allocation) in many schools which I visit.

5. A 'time blocked' approach for each genre is applied.

A two-to-three week block of time needs to be set aside so that each non-fiction genre has sufficient dedicated time for in-depth consideration. This has particular implications for schools taking a cross-curricular approach to literacy. If well-planned, cross-curricular literacy certainly raises standards. But if too many text types are 'covered' (across the curriculum) in the same short space of time, then the end result inhibits effective writing and can actually be the single most significant cause of genre-confusion.

6. Writing has real purposes and real audiences.

The final key pedagogic principle which should be discussed by **all** staff is how best to ensure the broadest possible range of real purposes and real audiences for writing. Many exciting opportunities now exist, such as peer reviewing of writing using shared 'Dropbox' (or other cloud-based) accounts; making links with other schools globally using LMYL (Lend Me Your Literacy) and Epals; blogging; class websites; writing to newspapers; producing a school magazine / e-zine etc.

KEY IMPROVEMENT TWO: SIMPLIFICATION OF THE LANGUAGE USED TO DESCRIBE EACH STRUCTURAL ELEMENT OF THE TEXT-TYPES

In the 2004 publication, the language used to describe each structural element of the non-fiction genres was most suitable for older/more able pupils. It was less appropriate for younger pupils. In this book we have addressed this issue and have sought to use the simplest possible language, without being reductive, to describe the structural elements of each genre. We have also carefully differentiated the language features so that 'mental working space' is not occupied learning unnecessarily complex terminology, but rather is freed up to focus on the key language features which actually engage the reader.

SUMMARY

To summarise, the aim of this new book is to assist schools aiming to implement a systematic, practical, whole-school approach to the teaching of non-fiction writing. The language used for the structural elements is deliberately simple, without being simplistic, whilst a developmental continuum is suggested for the associated language features of each genre.

This book has been co-authored with Mathew Sullivan, an outstanding full-time primary school teacher who has already co-authored other educational books with me. Mathew's input has transformed this publication - two heads have certainly been far better than one! In fact, for many of the following chapters, Mathew took the lead-writer's role.

We trust that the book will prove invaluable for both teachers and pupils.

Alan Peat and Mathew Sullivan
May 2015

INSTRUCTIONS

DEFINITION: An instructional text provides detailed information about how something should be done or operated.

PURPOSE: To provide the reader with clear, accessible, step-by-step guidelines which enable them to achieve a desired outcome, such as production (e.g. recipes), assembly (e.g. a Lego set), maintenance (e.g. a software upgrade), or activities (e.g. a board game).

AUDIENCE: Instructional texts are written for a range of widely varying audiences. Depending on the specifics of the intended outcome, the tone of the instructions might be modified, along with the style and formality of language used. In all cases, however, the unifying aims in instructional writing are **clarity** and **accuracy**.

SUGGESTED STIMULI & RELATED ACTIVITIES

Pupils may explore a range of existing stimuli and introductory activities, separated broadly into the areas we will use for the **method** aspect of the structural model:

How to make
Examples:
- Cookery recipes
- Creative projects
- Art models
- Furniture assembly

How to do
Examples:
- Using science equipment for investigations
- Finding your way
- Updating phone software
- Caring for an animal

How to play
Examples:
- Board game instructions
- Computer games
- Playground games
- Setting up computer consoles

Pupils may also explore the broad range of media which is currently used to convey instructions. In particular, video-streaming services like YouTube are fast becoming the most popular sources for instructional videos. This will provide pupils with a varied way of publishing their written work for a real audience.

There are also many effective warm-up games for instructional writing based on verbal instructions.

EXAMPLE: Two pupils sit back to back. Pupil A has a previously unseen image and Pupil B has a whiteboard. Pupil A has to verbally instruct Pupil B so that he/she replicates the image. At the end of the activity, both pupils evaluate the outcome and discuss how the instructions could be made more precise. They then swap roles and try to implement the improvements they have discussed.

STRUCTURAL MODEL

Pupil 'access' language	Meta language
1. Title	1. Title
2. What you are doing	2. Introductory paragraph outlining end goal
3. What you need	3. List of requirements or ingredients
4. How to make, do or play it	4. Clear, sequential method
5. How you know it's worked	5. Summative paragraph with success criteria
6. Tips / Extras	Additional helpful information

(Note: If pupils internalise the 'access language' of the structural model and can talk through this in sequence, they are free to concentrate on 'composition and effect' - this is the same for **all** linear non-fiction text types.)

Structural model part 1: Title

Titles should be clear and concise — leaving the reader in no doubt as to the function of the text (including the end goal).

Language features:

1. Verbing an object.

A simple, concise title which employs a continuous verb (an 'ing' ending action, drawn from the method) followed by the indefinite article 'a' or 'an', and then the object, or end goal, of the instructions:

Cooking a roast.

Building a model bridge.

Playing a game of snakes and ladders.

Drawing a comic.

2. How to _____

Another concise variant that explains the function of the text in a way that makes it clear that a **method** will be involved. It opens with the phrase 'How to', followed by a verb (action) and then the object, or end goal, of the instructions:

How to bake a chocolate cake.

How to make a bean bag.

How to assemble a table.

How to play dodgeball.

If the audience is known, the language complexity can be varied accordingly:

How to draw a tower.
(General audience)
vs.
How to create a proportionally accurate structural design.
(Specialist audience e.g. architecture student)

3. A guide to _____

This technique opens with the phrase 'A guide to' - language which may suit instructions which aim to support an under-confident or reluctant recipient. This 'softer' opening is then followed by a continuous verb ('ing' ending action), followed by the intended outcome of the instructions:

A guide to making paper planes.

A guide to painting a fence.

A guide to updating your phone.

A guide to using Facebook.

Variants of this 'softer' opening include:

Help to_____

Help to update your Twitter profile.

and

The way to_____

The way to make a tree house.

4. Joke or pun title

This title style depends on a knowledge of the intended audience, and it enables the writer to establish a more informal, relaxed tone. It provides the teacher with a useful variant for higher ability writers who are capable of confidently balancing personal writing and clear, formal instructions:

Internet searching for dummies!

Finding your way – a guide to your SatNav.

Bake like a pro!

Structural model part 2: What you are doing

This introductory element should include a brief summary of the intended outcome of the instructions. The purpose of this section is to simultaneously engage and prepare the reader. It should come under the sub-heading 'Introduction'.

Language features:

1. This guide _____

A simple starter, this technique opens with the phrase 'This guide', and continues with a brief summary of the objective of the instructions. It goes well with the 'to **verb** an **object**' title as a way to open an instructional text where the intended readership is unknown or very general:

This guide will help you to bake a delicious cake.

This guide contains instructions on how to update your PC.

This guide will show you how to build a chair.

2. Step-by-step

This opener is built around the key instructional phrase, 'step-by-step'. It assures the reader (and reminds the writer) that the text will contain clear, sequential instructions which, if followed correctly, will lead to the desired outcome:

This guide provides step-by-step instructions on how to clean your teeth.

These step-by-step instructions will help you create the perfect clay pot.

Follow these instructions, step-by-step, to build a sturdy bench.

3. 2A (two adjectives) Opener

This opener employs two adjectives in a list to describe the outcome (first example) the instructions (second example) or both (third example). It implicitly reassures the reader that the intended outcome will be achieved without wasted effort. Alternatively, it may give an indication of the desirability of the finished product. Or both at the same time.

Follow these instructions to create a delicious, moist Christmas pudding.

These clear, easy-to-use guidelines will help you to update your iPod.

This useful, straightforward guide will help you to make a speedy, aerodynamic paper plane.

4. Struggling to?

This technique draws the reader in with a rhetorical question which opens with the words 'Struggling to', followed by the intended outcome of the instructions. This is followed by a promise of assistance which leads the reader into the main body of the text:

Struggling to make a tasty fruit smoothie? This helpful guide will get you sorted!

Struggling to impress in the kitchen? Follow this guide to create a mouth-watering roast that no-one will forget!

Struggling to find what you want on the internet? Read this comprehensive guide to searching the web.

This supportive, friendly language technique could also be combined (where appropriate) with the '2A opener':

Struggling to impress in the kitchen? Follow this guide to create a mouth-watering, sumptuous roast that no-one will ever forget!

5. Time opener

This opener is useful when the task that follows appears arduous, as it works to negate that perception. Depending on the outcome and the process, the time element can be specific (first example) semi-specific (second example) or optimistically speculative (final example):

Follow this step-by-step guide to create a delicious dessert in only half an hour.

This guide will help you to cook the perfect roast chicken in under 40 minutes.

Follow these instructions and you will have a sturdy bed constructed in no time.

6. Congratulations on...!

Beginning with the phrase 'Congratulations on...', this amiable, engaging opener continues with an assurance that the instructions will help the reader get the most out of the product or project. This opener works particularly well for instructions for purchased items, as the language used fits a customer-producer dynamic:

Congratulations on buying a Bikea sofa! This is the most comfortable sofa on the market, and here's how to get the most out of it.

Congratulations on becoming an Hairfix model maker! Follow this guide to make a model that will impress all your friends.

Congratulations on taking up the challenge of Christmas dinner! These instructions will help you to make a holiday meal the family will talk about for years to come.

Another engaging, less formal variant is the 'Welcome opener':

Welcome to this guide to making the best fajitas in the world! You'll be in flavour-town in no time – follow the instructions and get going!

Welcome to your new grilling machine! Dive into a world of culinary perfection by following these simple, step-by-step instructions.

7. Before _____ing (the warning opener)

This cautionary opener is useful when the intended outcome could be hazardous (… if used or constructed improperly). It sets a professional, formal tone from the outset by opening with 'Before _____ing', ('____ing' being a verb drawn from the intended final outcome of the instructions):

Before using your BlendWhisk2000, please take the time to read through these important operating instructions.

Before building your new tree house, please read the following instructions carefully.

Before attempting to use a wok, you should read the following step-by-step instructions to avoid any fire damage to your kitchen.

Structural model part 3: What you need

This part of the instructional text is comprised of a comprehensive list of the ingredients, equipment or materials that the reader will need in order to achieve the end goal. They can be presented under a variety of sub-headings depending on the focus of the instructions, including: requirements, ingredients, materials, tools and/or equipment, essentials, or simply 'You will need'.

Language features:

1. List layout

There should be one item per line, separated with bullet points, numbers (numerical) or letters (alphabetical):

- *450g of haddock fillets.*
- *300ml milk.*
- *Half a lemon, sliced.*

1. *Cup.*
2. *Teabag.*
3. *Kettle.*

a. *20 Philips head screws.*
b. *12 2x4 plywood boards.*
c. *Hacksaw.*

As you can see, the choice of list punctuation often depends on what follows. For example, bullet points are a sensible choice for items that start with measurements, as this avoids numeric confusion.

2. Amounts and measurements

Use amounts and units of measure for appropriate items, allowing for cross-curricular numeracy discussion e.g.

- *6 x 12mm screws*

- *250ml honey*

- *10 ounces of paprika*

- *2lbs. minced beef*

3. 2A descriptions

Use two adjectives, separated by a comma, to provide specific information about items:

- *5 large, ripe bananas.*

- *a large, greased loaf tin.*

- *a small, serrated knife.*

4. Optional items

Extra items may be included in the list, which depend on the reader's individual need or preference. These may be presented after the main list as separate sentences (without bullet point punctuation) in order to identify them as optional:

A large serving tray may also be useful.

You may also need another person to help.

Adding the terms 'optional', 'as needed' or 'as required' demonstrates that these elements are not mandatory:

- *Paprika (as needed).*

- *Asparagus (if in season).*

- *Salt (to taste).*

Structural model part 4: How to make, do or play it

This section contains the actual instructions, in sequence, which the reader will follow in order to achieve the desired outcome. Again, it could be presented under a variety of subheadings depending on the purpose of the text, such as 'Method', 'What to do', 'Instructions', 'Procedure', 'Directions', 'Guidelines' etc.

(Note: each separate instruction should start on a new line.)

Language features:

1. Sequence word, action verb

Begin each new instruction with a sequential connective that positions it relative to the previous and next instruction, followed by a comma and an imperative verb linked to the necessary action for that step:

First, put…
Next, add…
After that, mix…
Once completed, stir in…
Then, heat…
Now, season…
Finally, serve…

Note that if the instructions are **numbered**, the sequential connective becomes redundant and should be omitted.

2. Two-step instructions

It may be appropriate in some cases for one instruction to contain two linked actions which are so interdependent that it would be detrimental to the outcome of the instructions to separate them:

Pour in the milk and stir until thoroughly mixed.

This could be extended using a '**With an action, more action**' sentence:

With a steady motion, fold the mixture until a dough forms.

Or an '**As ___ly**' sentence:

As you add the paint gradually, stir the mixture until the correct colour appears.

3. Consequence instructions

Some actions within instructions may depend on the outcome of others. You can demonstrate this using dependent terms:

Once the glue is set, stack the wood onto the base.

Stir the mixture until it has a creamy consistency.

If the surface is damp, use a sponge to soak up the water.

4. Adverbs of manner + verb

This technique accentuates **how** the action should be carried out by putting the adverb of manner first:

Slowly place the uranium in the container.

Carefully lift the test tube from the stand.

Gently remove the foil so as not to disturb the ingredients.

5. (Brackets for choices)

As in the 'what you need' section, some optional information or steps may be added within brackets:

(Add more salt if needed.)

(Repeat this step until the desired effect is achieved.)

As may helpful 'notes':

(Note: keep a close eye on the temperature as the mixture will heat up rapidly.)

And references to diagrams and/or equipment lists:

Insert screw A into hole B using the Allen key (see figure 8).

6. Italics *stressed word* instructions

Italics draw the reader's attention to critical aspects of the text:

Add the milk *before* the mixture starts to bubble.

Tighten screw A *after* putting the washer in place.

Tap the container *lightly* to loosen the contents.

(**Emboldening** and use of a different font colour achieve the same end.)

7. Object (aka)

Providing alternate names for equipment or ingredients helps to ensure that the instructions are understood by the widest possible audience:

Use a grill pan (aka a griddle) to fry the steak for two minutes on each side.

Use the gas torch (aka Bunsen Burner) to heat the mixture to 200°c.

Using an adjustable spanner (aka a wrench), tighten the bolt.

Structural model part 5: How you know it's worked

This summative section lets the reader know they have completed the process and provides them with a success criteria against which to gauge the final outcome. It is written in the form of a regular paragraph (no more bullet points) and can be presented under the subheading 'Summary'.

Language features:

1. When, then

This technique works by providing a success criteria which starts with the word 'When', and ends with a positive description of the outcome:

When the structure can support the weight of the books, then you will have an attractive, functional book shelf.

A variation of this technique is the '**if – then**' summary:

If you have followed these instructions accurately, then you should have a sturdy, functional work desk.

2. Now summaries

This technique acknowledges the completion of the process (using the adverb 'now') and presents a success criteria against which to measure the outcome:

Now you will have a filling, warming soup for that special Bonfire Night party.

You will now have a finished paper plane, ready to be launched on its first test flight.

You should now have a completed bookcase, ready to fill with your favourite reads.

3. Most important – in short summary

This summary includes a list of success criteria, followed by the key criteria for the reader to check their outcome against:

The cake should be light, fluffy and moist – in short, delicious!

The structure should be strong, stable and durable – in short, a reliable storage solution.

The tea should be hot, aromatic and golden brown – in short, a lovely brew!

4. Exclamation summary

This informal summary utilises exclamation marks, and has a more congratulatory tone than the previous techniques (it also **assumes** success). As such, it is most appropriately used when the activity is fun. There are a few variants:

Congratulations!

Congratulations! You have just made your very own tiara!

Sound! + result

Ta daah! Your culinary masterpiece is complete and ready to serve!

What + !

What an amazing result! Enjoy using your new dining table!

Structural model part 6: Tips / Extras

This final section is not mandatory, but does serve to add authenticity to instruction writing (particularly for more able writers) by incorporating the same types of contextual, follow-up, and/or health and safety ideas that are found in real-life examples of the genre. It may be presented under a variety of subheadings depending on the content, such as 'Tips', 'Additional Information', 'Health and Safety', 'Advice', etc.

Language features:

I. For best results,

Provides additional information on how to get the most out of the final outcome:

For best results, serve the dessert ice cold.

For best results, consume within five days.

For best results, add cream and serve with sweet biscuits.

2. Optional extras

Informs readers of potential 'add-ons' that will further improve the outcome:

If you want to extend the life of your newly-built fence, give it a coat of Bigronseal.

If you want to spice up the dish, add a dash of paprika.

If you wish to improve the flight of the plane, try adding extra foils on the wings.

3. Safety tips

These can be integrated into the '**How to make, do or play it**' or the '**How you know it's worked**' sections of the text:

When using the flame thrower, make sure you are accompanied by an adult.

When removing the tray from the oven, make sure you wear oven mitts.

When fuelling the lawnmower, be sure to avoid naked flames.

4. Follow-up ideas

This technique presents the reader with concrete ways to further expand, modify or add to the outcome once it is completed:

You could change the colour of the cake by adding four drops of your desired colour of food dye before mixing.

You could customise the shoe rack by adding a coat of paint.

You may wish to periodically switch the contents of the vase to match the season and keep it looking fresh.

5. Troubleshooting

Here, the writer predicts or acknowledges any issues with the process and pre-empts them with potential solutions:

If you find that the plane does not fly straight, try bending the wing sections up or down until the flight issue is resolved.

6. Extra information source

To mirror modern instructions and make reference to external information, simply include a reference to a real or invented website:

For more delicious recipes, visit www.chubbycakes.com

To view a video tutorial of this activity, go to www.diymasters.com

For guides on further experiments, check out www.sciencemad.com

7. Nutritional information

Appropriate specifically for food instructions, this allows links to be made to science and PSHE for healthy eating:

One cornflake cake contains 4.9g of fat, 13.5g of sugar and 150 calories (8% RDA).

Free Phone Calls Forever!
How to make tin-can telephones

This guide will show you how to make your very own set of tin-can phones. Follow the step-by-step instructions to create a fun toy which can carry your voice to a friend: you won't even get a phone bill at the end of the day! Before attempting to build your own tin-can phones, make sure you read this guide carefully, as some parts of the process could be dangerous. Let's begin…

What you need
(a) 2 clean, empty, tin cans (with lids removed)
(b) A length of thick string (about 6 metres to start)
(c) A nail
(d) A hammer
(e) A permanent marker
(f) Electrical tape
(g) Paint and decorating materials (optional)

What to do
Firstly, turn one of the tin cans upside down, and use the permanent marker to mark the centre of the circular face.

Secondly, with an adult's supervision, hold the nail so that the point rests on the mark, then use the hammer to drive the nail through the tin. (*Don't* hammer the nail all the way through: leave about an inch sticking out)

After that, *carefully* take hold of the end of the nail that is sticking out, and remove it. If the nail is stuck, use the claw part of the hammer to prise it out.

Next, repeat the first three steps for the other tin can. Once completed, you should have two empty, lidless tin cans with holes in the bottom faces.

Now, avoiding any sharp edges, take one end of the string and thread it carefully through the hole in one of the cans, from the bottom to the open top (if there are any dangerous, sharp edges, use the electrical tape to cover them).

After that, tie a knot in the end of the string large enough to block up the hole. If you test the string and it slips through, simply re-thread it and double the knot. Repeat these steps for the other can. You now have a complete set of tin-can phones!

How you know it's worked
Hold one of the tin-can phones, while your friend takes the other and moves as far away as the string will allow. Hold the open end of the tin can over your ear while your friend talks into the other, making sure the string is pulled tight all the while. When you hear their voice, carried through the string, and they hear yours, then you know your tin-can phones work. What an amazing result! Free phone calls forever!

Tips & Extras
You could use paint and decorating materials to personalise your tin-can phones. You could also test their range by replacing the string with a longer length. Why not see how far apart you and your friend can be while still able to hear each other?

To learn more about how tin-can telephones work, visit *www.lovemyscience.com/tincanphone*

RECOUNT

DEFINITION: A recount is a retelling of a factual or fictional event. A 'faction' recount blends fact and fiction.

PURPOSE: To inform and/or entertain a reader.

AUDIENCE: Recounts are written for a wide variety of audiences. These may be known or unknown to the writer. If known, the intended audience will have a direct bearing on both the style and formality of language used.

SUGGESTED STIMULI & RELATED ACTIVITIES

The range of stimuli or introductory activities for recounts can be very broad. It is therefore useful to think of recounts in three distinct categories, each of which has its own specific stimuli:

1. Recounts which are factual (based on real events the pupil has experienced).

Stimuli or activities for such recounts may include:

A school trip - to a theatre, art gallery, museum etc.

A famous person's visit to the school.

An extended field trip - outdoor education weekend, climbing school etc.

2. Recounts which are fictional (based on 'made-up' events)

Stimuli / activities for such recounts may include:

Watching an excerpt from a science fiction film. For example, as a stimulus for a recount titled 'A visit to Earth in 3000 A.D.' in which the writer may wish to draw on the film for detail and orientation.

Reading an excerpt from an explorer's story, then assuming the character of the explorer to write a recount of the ascent of a mountain.

Looking at a picture of a fantasy environment (Pandora from *Avatar*, for example) and using it as a stimulus for a recount of a visit to that location.

3. 'Faction' (blending fact and fiction) recounts

Stimuli or activities for such recounts include the reading of a selection of primary and secondary source materials related to a specific historical event, for instance 'The Battle of the Somme'. Pupils then write the recount as if they were an eyewitness (fictional) but include accurate historical details derived from the sources (factual) = 'faction'!

STRUCTURAL MODEL

Pupil 'access' language	Meta language
I. All the W's (When? Who? Where? What? Why?)	I. Succinct overview paragraph
2. Before we...	2. Description of planning stage of the activity
3. First, next, then, finally (only interesting!)	3. Sequential description of the *significant* events (avoiding bland procedural elements)
4. What I/we thought*	4. Personalised evaluations of events (continuing in sequence)
5. Main points / most interesting	5. Summative/evaluative ending

* When introducing this text type to younger pupils, it is wise to have this as a stand-alone element at this point in the recount. For older learners, the teacher should encourage the integration of personalised evaluation throughout the entire sequential report.

(Note: If pupils internalise the 'access language' of the structural model and can talk through this in sequence then they are free to concentrate on composition and effect - this is the same for **all** linear non-fiction text types.)

Structural model part 1: All the W's

The opening paragraph of a simple recount is always an *overview* paragraph.

Language features:

The simplest way to teach this is for **all** staff to describe it as a **5w's paragraph,** the five W's being:

When? Who? Where? What? Why?

The order of the W's is fundamentally important. For younger pupils a focus on complex sentences, which include the word 'because', is essential as this is the **bridging word** which links the final two W's - What? & Why?

The following examples of 5W's paragraphs demonstrate the essential use of the word 'because' as part of the paragraph's conclusion:

*Last week our class went to the museum to look at some old toys **because** we have been learning about the Victorians.*

*Yesterday a circus group visited our school **because** we have been learning about circuses.*

*On Monday I went to the aquarium with my family **because** I wanted to learn more about sharks.*

With older pupils the structure of the 5W's paragraph does NOT change, though the language content becomes more sophisticated:

*Last week Class 6b visited The Manchester Museum in order to study and handle a broad range of artefacts. The visit was useful **because** we have only been able to consider secondary source material in the classroom, and we wanted to handle objects from the historical period being studied.*

- Factual recount

*Seven rotations ago, Strike Group Alpha was mobilised and ordered to report for a briefing. Our mission was to explore the hostile planet of Beta Prime, **because** it was believed to have rich deposits of our most precious resource, Hydrotron.*

- Fictional recount

*On August 24th, at about midday, Vesuvius began spewing volcanic ash and stone far up into the sky. Even though we had been given warnings, we didn't leave **because** the volcano had never troubled us before.*

- 'Faction' recount

Whatever the ability of the writer, this initial paragraph should not contain too much detail (the paragraph is an overview). If necessary, consider setting a three-sentence limit. As there are 5W's, this constraint will compel pupils to combine simple sentences to form complex and/or compound sentences.

Structural model part 2: Before we...

This relatively short section considers the preparation stage for the event which is being recounted. The element title (Before we…) relates to the position of the writing segment relative to the main body, i.e. *'before we* (**main event**), we (**prepared**)'. The purpose of this section is usually to set the scene, or to provide the audience with important information.

The key points to emphasise are **relevancy** and **interest**. When writing a recount of a class rock climbing trip, for example, a reader would need to know about the specialised climbing equipment that had to be checked and packed in preparation. They would not, however, need to know about the cucumber and ham sandwiches that were also packed. Remind pupils to ask themselves before they write: **is it relevant, and is it interesting?** Is it something the reader would need to know if planning a similar trip?

Language features:

1. Time starters

As recounts are organised chronologically, consider providing useful, time-based sentence starters to help pupils with this sequential formatting:

Before we went...
Before setting out…

Previously…
Three hours before…
Prior to…
Initially…
That morning…
etc.

An hour before we were due to depart, our team captain called us together for a meeting about tactics.

- Sports competition recount

Prior to departing, we passed through the security gate, where all our belongings were checked by an x-ray scanner.

- School trip recount

Initially we were due to land in the Ocean of Serenity, but due to reports of stellar storms, we modified our plans and located another spot for touch down.

- Fictional recount

2. Some; others

Usually, a recount will refer to the actions of more than one individual (i.e. individuals other than the writer or the character assumed by the writer). The 'Some; others' sentence type allows the writer to comment succinctly on the simultaneous, perhaps even conflicting, preparatory actions of other people involved in the event, through the use of two clauses joined by a semi-colon:

Some of the team listened to music to psyche themselves up; others preferred to sit in silence.

- Sports competition recount

Some of the soldiers cleaned their weapons; others helped to load ammunition onto the trucks.

- 'Faction' recount

Some of the parents cried as they waved at their children; others couldn't wait for them to leave!

- School trip recount

3. (Verb)ed next (Verb)ed

This sentence type reinforces the sequential, often cause-and-effect, patterning of recount writing by presenting two linked, dependent actions (in the form of past tense verbs, hence the 'ed' ending reminder):

I clambered excitedly out of bed and hurried to pack my things.

- Scouts trip recount

We travelled to base camp and received our safety instructions from the officer in charge.

- Exploration recount

Once the pupils are confident in their writing of this sentence type, it is important to explain that not every past-tense verb ends in 'ed':

*I **shot** down the road and **flung** myself onto the waiting bus.*

- School trip recount

4. Outside (inside)

A long list of sequential actions does not make for an engaging recount! This technique helps the writer to include insights into their own feelings, an effective break from the 'first, next, then' structure:

As we prepared to leave school I tried to look brave for my mum. (Inside, however, I wanted to cry: I was going to miss her.)

- School trip recount

I looked as determined and confident as possible while listening to our new orders. (Yet inside I was trembling and wondering what monstrous beings might be out there.)

- Fictional adventure recount

I tried to appear as calm as possible for my little girl. (Inside, though, I was numb with fear: the warnings were too late.)

- 'Faction' recount

5. List sentences

Lists of equipment, lists of people, lists of destinations, and so on, are often included in recounts. Simple lists can be constructed with single words or short phrases, separated by commas:

I packed my goggles, skis, boots, helmet and scarf.

- Family holiday recount

We packed the laser guns, grenade launchers, binoculars, rations and medical supplies.

- Fictional recount

…or expanded phrases, which are separated using semi colons:

On the team was Ian, the forensic scientist; Jane, the marine biologist; Martin, the officer in charge of safety; and me, the behavioural scientist.

- Fictional adventure recount

We planned the safest route: up past the boulder fields; down the ravine; through the tunnels; then the final ascent up the cliff face.

- Adventure holiday recount

(Note: Techniques 2 - 5 would also be appropriate for use in the main body of the recount.)

Structural model part 3: First, next, then, finally (only interesting!)

This is the main body of the text: the key events are recounted **in the order that they occurred**. Once again, the writer should ensure that the content is **interesting**. This is achieved through the careful selection and sequential arrangement of the most **relevant, engaging** details.

Language features:

1. First, next, then

The structural element title '**First, next, then**' contains the temporal connectives which pupils can use to ensure that the recount is sequential. They may be placed at the start of paragraphs, thereby demonstrating a time-shift:

First we travelled from the base camp towards the start of the ascent. The mountain towered ahead of us, growing larger and larger as we...

Next, we unloaded our gear and attached our harnesses to the cams at the base of the cliff, checking our ropes while...

Then we began to climb in pairs, the lead climber setting new cam holds as their partners belayed from below...

- Fictional adventure recount

2. BOYS

'BOYS' is a useful acronym that reminds pupils of a range of connectives they could include throughout their work:

But   The visiting magician performed plenty of tricks, **but** everyone shouted for him to do more.

Or   We needed to get out of there at once, **or** we would have been trapped in the path of the ash.

Yet   Jack was clearly a proficient skater, **yet** he chose not to show off.

So   The first round of gunfire had proved effective, **so** the general ordered the troops to fire again.

3. De: de
(Description: detail)

This versatile sentence structure enables the writer to describe an element of the event being recounted, then expand upon it with extra relevant and interesting details:

The rock face was intimidating: the surface glimmered with slippery ice and smooth stone.

- Fictional adventure recount

The room we stayed in was less than pleasant: cockroaches scurried across the floor and the ceiling was blistered with water from the leaking roof.

- Holiday recount

4. Noun, who/which/where,

This sentence type allows the writer to expand on descriptive details via the inclusion of a subordinate clause containing additional relevant information about the **subject**. This clause begins with 'who', 'which', or 'where', and is situated after the noun.

The museum, which had four floors of exhibits, was filled with a wide variety of resources to help our learning.

- School trip recount

Captain Brown, who was the leader of our company, was the first one over the enemy wall.

- 'Faction' recount

The northern route, where the river ran quickest, proved to be the best way to reach the camp.

- Scout trip recount

5. Position + place, subject + action

The efficacy of many recounts depends just as much on the reader being able to imagine and orientate himself/herself mentally in the **location** that the writer is describing as it does on the reader being able to follow the **events**. This sentence type enables the writer to situate the reader clearly in the location (position + place), before moving smoothly into a description of what occurred there (subject + action):

On the back row of the hot, crowded bus, I got travel sick and vomited all over Jamie Smith.

- *Scout trip recount*

High above the canopy layer, our helicopters hovered as we looked for a way to penetrate the dense foliage.

- *Adventure recount*

On the top floor of the museum, we looked at the remains of a real mummy!

- *School trip recount*

6. Emotion – consequence

As mentioned in the explanation of the Outside (inside) method (See page 36), the inclusion of the writer's emotions, or even the emotions of those around them, often adds variety to the recount of a series of linked events. The 'Emotion – consequence' technique combines an emotional insight with a description of the consequence of that emotion:

Our instructor was angry – he shouted at us until we did as he said.

- *School trip recount*

I was terrified – I held on to the rudder and steered as hard as I could to escape the terrifying rapids.

- *Scout trip recount*

We were mesmerised – we watched the strange, alien creature in silence as it disappeared into the forest.

- *Fictional adventure recount*

7. 3 adjectives _ed

This sentence type affords the writer a succinct way of integrating emotional details into descriptions of action without disrupting the flow of a recount. It begins with a list of three adjectives (ending in 'ed') separated by commas, before concluding with a description of the event that has caused the emotional response:

Frightened, confused, abandoned, we clambered through the dark caves, searching for a way to escape.

- Fictional adventure recount

Delighted, enthralled, captivated, we waited with baited breath to see the performer's next trick.

- School visit recount

Once the composition of this technique has been grasped it is important to show pupils that not all emotional adjectives end in 'ed':

Cold, wet, miserable, we climbed up the final stage of the cliff and finally reached the summit.

- Adventure recount

8. Description, action

This sentence type opens with a subordinate clause, thereby inverting the typical sentence structure used by many pupils. It starts with a description of the subject, then continues after a comma to the main clause, where the linked action is conveyed:

Being the bravest member of the group, Jack volunteered to go first.

- School trip recount

As the leader of the regiment, Colonel Jack organised the offensive.

- 'Faction' recount

As I was the smallest boy in the group, I was told to go into the cave first.

- Scout trip recount

9. Finally

After having recounted the main events using the 'First, next, then,' sequence, the temporal connective 'Finally' can now be used, followed by the description of one or two ultimate actions:

Finally we returned to the camp after four long days of trekking. I was glad to see my bed and I fell asleep as soon as my head touched the pillow.

- Scout trip recount

Finally the cast took a bow and we stood up and applauded. Our teacher led us out of the theatre and we travelled home on the bus, chatting about the performance all the way.

- School trip recount

Finally we spotted the rescue helicopter: we were saved. We helped the injured soldiers to climb on board, then we clambered in and set off home.

- Fictional adventure recount

Structural model part 4: What I/we thought

This section needn't always be separate from the above; more confident and developed writers may integrate their evaluation of an event with the presentation of the event as it arises sequentially. However, for introductory purposes, it is useful to remind pupils to provide reflection on their experiences at the end of a recount.

Language features:

1. What I liked and why

In this section, pupils should include a description of the most interesting element of the visit, activity or day. This should have only been mentioned briefly in their writing, or not mentioned at all. Pupils will then explain their choice (the '**why**') using words like 'because' or 'as':

I really liked the juggling clowns because I am learning to juggle myself, and it was good to see it done properly.

- School visit recount

I loved the white-water rapids as they were fast and exciting, but I never felt scared.

- School trip recount

This idea can also be expanded to cover what the writer **did not** like, and why (evaluations can, of course, be negative as well as positive):

I could not stand the humidity on that hostile planet as it made me feel like I was struggling to breathe.

- Fictional adventure recount

As pupils progress, more sophisticated language, such as 'preferred', 'engaging', 'particularly', 'interesting' etc. may be introduced. Positive and negative opinions can also be presented **simultaneously** using a '**BOYS**' sentence (See page 38):

*I did not particularly care for the static exhibits because I had seen them before, **yet** I found handling the sceptre extremely engaging, as it made me feel like a king!*

- School trip recount

Pupils could also consider using 2A sentences (two adjectives before a noun) for descriptive passages:

I loved the long, warm days because they allowed us to see and do so much, but I did not care for the loud, crowded subways as they made travelling quite uncomfortable.

- Holiday recount

Specific stylistic features should also be modelled, e.g. the use of bullet points for key points:

As I am a person who loves adventure, I particularly enjoyed:
- *Climbing the ice ledge during the ascent*
- *Having to fix the boat while on the move*
- *Almost getting stuck in a very small cavern!*

Structural model part 5: Main points/ most interesting

The conclusion of a recount should be both **summative** and **evaluative**. The teacher should model and stress the need for both of these elements. It is also important to remember that in this section writers should be evaluating the **overall experience**, rather than individual experiences (as in the previous section).

Language features:

1. Reword

Key points made earlier in the recount are rephrased and shortened for succinctness so that they can contribute to an **overall** summary of the event. The technique should be modelled, ensuring pupils do not merely repeat what they have written previously:

Previous sentence:
Initially we were due to land in the Ocean of Serenity, but due to reports of stellar storms, we modified our plans and located another spot for touchdown.

Rephrased sentence:
We had to change our plans, but the landing worked out well.

Previous sentence:
The room we stayed in was less than pleasant: cockroaches scurried across the floor and the ceiling swelled with water from the leaking roof.

New sentence:
Our room was most unpleasant, for reasons I would rather not repeat.

2. Overall

This method opens with a summative phrase (e.g. 'Overall it was…', 'All in all…', 'Everything considered…' etc.) and then continues with a linked evaluative comment:

Overall it was a positive experience: I faced my fears and have grown in confidence, even if I had to share my bedroom with cockroaches!

- Scout trip recount

All in all, the battle was a success. Although many brave men died, the freedom of our country was secured.

- 'Faction' recount

Everything considered, the visit was one of the best I have ever been on. I will definitely be going back to the museum in the school holidays.

- School trip recount

3. In the end (time)

This technique is based on the same summative and evaluative structure as the previous one, though this time-based summative phrase gives the reader a sense of **finality**, clearly signalling the end of the recount:

At the end of the day, the team played extremely well and deserved their place on the podium.

- Sporting event recount

When all was said and done, the mission had been a failure. The dangerous life form was out of quarantine, and we had suffered major casualties.

- Fictional adventure recount

After all we had been through, the group came out stronger and more close-knit than ever. The trip was a great success.

- Scout trip recount

Mount Vesuvius: the Sleeping Giant Awakes

Yesterday, which was August 24th, 79 AD, the great Mount Vesuvius violently erupted, spewing so much scalding ash into the heavens that the sky over Pompeii became as black as night. Although we had been given warnings, we never really considered leaving: the volcano had never troubled us... until that fateful day.

Prior to yesterday, Vesuvius had been a calm, silent giant in our midst: we believed it to be dormant. We were so sure of the safety of the region that we created a thriving community in Pompeii, including an amphitheatre, a gymnasium, a port for ships and even a complex water system. On occasion, we did experience earthquakes. One particularly large quake occurred seventeen years ago, causing a substantial amount of damage in the region. Another took place two years later, although it is said that the emperor Nero, who was singing in the theatre at the time, did not even stop his performance. Some people also pointed out the flames at the top of the peak; most did not even notice this, nor did they know what it, and the quaking earth, signified, until it was too late.

On the morning of the 24th, by some good fortune, I packed my brushes, bottles and canvas, travelled to the Bay of Naples, and sailed to Misenum, in order that I might spend the day practising my landscape painting. Up high on a grassy hillside, I set up my equipment and looked back at the great Mount Vesuvius. It was about midday, when suddenly the volcano exploded violently, throwing up a fiery, smoky column, from which a choking ash began to fall. That was just the start...

As the hours passed, the thick, volcanic clouds rained down burning pumice, which I later discovered built up to depths of almost ten feet at Pompeii. Petrified, anxious, devastated, I watched as the ash darkened the sky and columns of fire shot up all around the volcano. I tried to fix my gaze, steady my hand, and record what I witnessed (yet inside I shook with dread, and an awful sadness at the inevitable loss of so many innocent souls completely overtook me).

Some days later, I would discover that after the first storms of pumice had fallen, pyroclastic flows (which are rivers of hot ash, pumice, rock fragments and volcanic gas) had rushed down the side of the volcano at tremendous speeds. These engulfed Pompeii, burning and asphyxiating anyone who remained. I was sickened – I did not move from my place on the hillside for a day, a night and another day. I felt rooted to the spot, like a petrified tree, unable to move and barely able to believe what I saw.

Finally, after days of waiting, some brave people ventured back to the city. Yet unlike the earthquakes of years gone by, where repair work would start almost straight away, no-one thought the city of Pompeii could be salvaged. In a way, I count my blessings that I decided to take the painting trip that morning, yet the pain of the loss of so many loved ones haunts me still.

In the end, while some explorers tunnel away to save what they can from the site, I have decided never to return. The tragedy of Vesuvius is burned into my memory in fire and ash and I shall recount it no more after this.

EXPLANATIONS

DEFINITION: An account or commentary that makes something clear by describing the relevant structure, operation or circumstances.

PURPOSE: To tell the reader how something works or to clarify what causes something to happen, through reason and analysis.

AUDIENCE: Written for a variety of audiences, on a range of subjects, so content should be as accessible as possible. However, some technical language may be used, in which case the writer should ensure that any jargon is used in context and explained.

SUGGESTED STIMULI & RELATED ACTIVITIES

Children may explore a range of existing stimuli or introductory activities, separated broadly into the three explanation 'sub-genres':

Explanation of a process
Examples:
Life cycle.
Industrial processes (e.g. recycling).
Hibernation.
Water cycle.

How things work
Examples:
Earth, Sun and Moon system.
The human eye.
Engines.
Food production.

Why something happened
Examples:
The sinking of the Titanic.
The destruction of Pompeii and Herculaneum.
The Moon landing.
The Hindenburg disaster.

These stimuli should be provided via a range of media, including documentary-based videos, many of which can be found on streaming services like YouTube. The 'How it Works' programmes, available to watch for free on YouTube, provide fascinating, fact-rich explanations of many different processes. In terms of 'Why something happened' explanations, National Geographic's website and their YouTube channel also provide plenty of useful mini-documentaries on a wide range of subjects.

A range of speaking and listening games can also be used to introduce the topic of explanations. One such game involves choosing an object, person or thing, writing it on a Post-it note and sticking it, unseen, onto a hat worn by a pupil. The other pupils in the class then take turns to explain the word to the hat-wearer, **without** using the word itself. The class keep track of the number of explanations given before the person guesses what is written on the Post-it note. They then try to better this score on their next attempt.

Note: The three types of explanation texts, and the techniques that are appropriate to them, will be identified using the following colour coding throughout this chapter:

Explanation of a process
How things work
Why something happened

STRUCTURAL MODEL:
Explanation of a process **and** How things work

Pupil 'access' language	Meta language
1. Title	1. Title
2. What this is about	2. General statement clarifying what the explanation will cover
3. What it needs	3. Further explanation of the general statement, including stages/parts
4. What happens/How it works	4. Sequential explanation with key points
5. What happens next or something interesting	5. Summative paragraph, including interesting facts

STRUCTURAL MODEL:
Why something happened

Pupil 'access' language	Meta language
1. Title	1. Title
2. What this is about	2. General statement clarifying what the explanation will cover
3. What *was* happening	3. Provision of contextual details
4. What happened and why	4. Explanation with key points developed via cause and effect
5. What happened next or something interesting	5. Summative paragraph, including interesting facts

(Note: If pupils internalise the 'access language' of the structural models and can talk through this in sequence, then they are free to concentrate on composition and effect - this is the same for **all** linear non-fiction text types.)

Structural model part 1: Title
For: Explanation of a process / How things work / Why something happened

Titles should be simultaneously clear and engaging – they provide an opportunity to inform the reader of the subject of the explanation **and** stimulate their curiosity.

Language features:

1. 5 W's / H?
For: Explanation of a process / How things work / Why something happened

This technique employs a rhetorical question beginning with one of the 5 W's (Who, What, When, Where, Why) or the H (How) to engage the reader via the implied promise of an answer:

How does a chicken grow?

How does the water cycle work?

Why did the Titanic sink?

Once this starter is understood, pupils may endeavour to make the question more open-ended or evocative whilst still hinting at the topic, thereby intriguing the reader:

How does an egg become an egg-maker?

Why do we need umbrellas?

Why did the unthinkable happen to the unsinkable?

2. The_____process/cycle/system
For: Explanation of a process

A simple title that makes the type of explanation clear by combining the subject with an appropriate key word:

The water **cycle.**

The recycling **process.**

The digestive **system.**

3. How a/n_____works
For: How things work

Another simple, accessible approach which leaves no room for confusion as it combines the subject with the key word 'works':

How a human eye **works.**

How an engine **works.**

How a wristwatch **works.**

4. Subject: explained / how it works / why it happened
For: Explanation of a process / How things work / Why something happened

This technique opens with a to-the-point subject title, then a colon, followed by the purpose of the text:

Hibernation: explained.

The Earth, Sun and Moon system: how it works.

The Hindenburg disaster: why it happened.

This technique could easily be extended with a tag question to engage the reader further:

Hibernation: why do animals do it?

The Earth, Sun and Moon system: where are we headed?

The Hindenburg disaster: what caused this tragedy?

5. A guide to_____
For: How things work

This title implies that the following text will be a helpful explanatory guide and is apt for when the writing purpose is to support a target audience which is relatively unfamiliar with the topic:

A guide to car engines.

A guide to the human heart.

A guide to mobile phones.

6. A _____'s journey
For: Explanation of a process

The implied anthropomorphism of this title makes it most suitable for texts in which the author makes use of personification to explain a process, making it sound like an exciting adventure:

A raindrop's journey.

A blood cell's journey.

A soda bottle's journey.

7. Alliteration + 5W's/H subheading
For: Explanation of a process / How things work / Why something happened

This more advanced, two-part title format uses alliteration to grab the reader's attention, with a subheading to make the subject of the explanation clear:

Busy Bees!
How honey is made.

Tick-Tock-Time
What *makes a watch work?*

Hindenburg Horror!
Why *the airship* **voyage ended in catastrophe.**

8. Exploring _____
For: Explanation of a process / How things work / Why something happened

By opening with the word 'exploring', this title variant implies that the text will be a collaborative voyage of discovery – involving and engaging the reader:

Exploring *the human respiratory system.*

Exploring *the Solar System.*

Exploring *the Moon landing.*

9. The truth/facts behind _____
For: Why something happened

This title frames the topic as a mystery, whilst implying that the writer has something authoritative or novel to say on the subject:

The truth behind *crop circles.*

The facts behind *the death of Tutankhamun.*

The facts behind *the disappearance of Amelia Earhart.*

Structural Model part 2: What this is about

This introductory section should include an overview of the explanation's subject (without giving away too much explanatory detail). It may be presented under the subheading 'Introduction'.

Language features:

1. Noun, who/which/where,
For: Explanation of a process / How things work / Why something happened

Opening with the subject of the explanation (the noun), this introductory sentence goes on to include a subordinate clause (who/which/where,) which provides extra information about the subject. It then concludes with information that leads the reader into the main body of the text:

The frog, which is an amphibious creature, starts its life underwater.

The Solar System, where our own home planet is located, operates in a complex and beautiful way.

The Titanic, which was completed in 1912, was the largest ship afloat at the time it was launched.

2. Time, details
For: Why something happened

When explaining why an important event happened, historical and chronological context is of critical importance. This opener establishes the time and/or date of the event first, then continues with the basic details of the event itself:

Built in 1936, the Hindenburg was a large, luxurious airship.

On 28 June 1914, Gavrilo Princip assassinated Archduke Franz Ferdinand of Austria, prompting World War I.

At 02.56 UTC on July 21st, 1969, Neil Armstrong became the first man to walk on the Moon.

3. 2A Opener
For: Explanation of a process / How things work / Why something happened

This opener employs two adjectives in a list to describe an aspect of the topic in a general way:

*The process of mummification included some **gruesome, invasive** procedures.*

*Tea is produced in **vast, impressive** quantities in numerous countries.*

*World War II was a **devastating, violent** conflict which caused the deaths of millions.*

4. The/A__(PROCESS)___ takes__(TIME)___.
For: Explanation of a process

This opening technique emphasises the timescale of a process as a key introductory component:

The life cycle of a frog takes between 12 and 16 weeks.

The process of brushing your teeth should take about three minutes.

A full Earth orbit of the Sun takes 365.25 days.

5. Then and now
For: How things work)

This introductory technique works by providing details about whatever **preceded** the subject that is being explained (**Then**) in order to show development and progression (**Now**):

*In the 19th Century, steam-powered engines were the height of technological advancement. **Now,** people all over the world rely on internal combustion to power their modes of transport.*

*In the 1980s, VHS tapes were used to watch films at home. **Now,** Blu-Ray disc players give audiences everywhere a high-definition viewing experience.*

Aristotle once claimed that the Sun orbited the Earth. **Now** we know that Earth is part of a heliocentric model.

6. Statement of fact. The question is:
For: Explanation of a process / How things work / Why something happened

This technique combines a factual statement with a question which goes to the heart of the whole explanation process. It stimulates the reader's interest and encourages critical, analytical thought:

Tea is consumed all over the world. **The question is: how is it made?**

Televisions are a common feature in homes all over the world. **The question is: how do they work?**

The Gunpowder Plot almost destroyed a monarchy. **The question is: what motivated the men behind it?**

7. Categorisation
For: Explanation of a process / How things work / Why something happened

This informative opener uses a range of phrases to categorise the subject, providing contextual information for the subsequent explanation:

Explanation of a process:

The frog **belongs to** *a largely carnivorous group called 'amphibians'.*
The water cycle **is an important part of** *the global ecosystem.*

How things work:

The blender **is a type of** *electric kitchen utensil.*
The aeroplane **is a mode of** *aerial transportation.*

Why something happened:

The Moon landing **was an historic** *event in American history.*
The assassination of John Lennon **was a tragic** *event of the 1980's.*

Structural model part 3: What it needs / Parts / What *was* happening

For: Explanation of a process / How things work / Why something happened

The content of this part of the text varies dramatically across the three explanation sub-genres. Therefore each will be addressed in its own discrete section.

Note: This section is not mandatory: there will be contexts in which the inclusion of this section would be inappropriate.

Structural model part 3: What it needs

For: Explanation of a process

This section serves to inform the reader of the different 'parts' or 'stages' of the process in general terms, providing an overview before the extrapolation of each part in the subsequent 'What happens' section.

Language features:

1. Process steps: list

This listing technique opens with the name of the process that is being explained, followed by the number of the steps or stages. It then introduces a list of these steps or stages using a colon:

The mummification process consists of three main stages: organ removal, drying and embalming.

2. Steps process: list

Working in a similar way to the previous example, this technique prioritises the **number** of steps, rather than the process, but finishes in the same manner:

*There are four main stages in the **water cycle: evaporation, condensation, precipitation and infiltration.***

3. The question is:

If this technique has not already been used, it is useful as a way of expanding this section and linking fluidly to the next element of the explanation:

*The mummification process consists of three main stages: organ removal, drying and embalming. **The question is: what exactly happened in each of these stages?***

*There are four main stages in the water cycle: evaporation, condensation, precipitation and infiltration. **The question is: how do these stages link together?***

Structural model part 3: Parts
For: How things work

In the 'How things work' sub-genre, this section lists the 'parts' that are required for the subject to function.

Language features:

1. Subject parts: list

This listing technique opens with the subject of the explanation, followed by a statement detailing the number of component parts. It then concludes with the names of each part:

The *human eye **consists of four main parts:** cornea, pupil, iris and lens.*

2. Subject stages: list

This technique differs from the previous one in that it focuses on the smaller functions that contribute to the larger working procedure:

*The internal combustion engine works in **three main stages:** intake, combustion and output.*

3. Requirements

This listing technique frames the component list as **non-negotiable elements** of the working procedure:

*An aeroplane **needs the following things to work:** thrust, gravity, lift and drag.*

*A kettle **needs the following things to work:** a power supply, water, and an operator.*

Structural model part 3: What was happening
For: Why something happened

The 'Why something happened' sub-genre does not require a list of component parts or requirements. Instead, a scene-setting, informative paragraph may be used to establish historical and/or social context, and tell the reader about how things were *prior* to the event that is being explained.

Language features:

1. Some; others

This technique presents two opposing views which existed before the focal event of the explanation:

***Some** thought the young pharaoh untouchable; **others** had different ideas.*

2. De: de

This technique opens with a description, followed by a key clarifying detail:

During the Blitz, children from London were evacuated en masse: they were taken to safe locations in the countryside.

3. Name – adjective pair –

This technique presents information in a main clause, separated by dashes to include a further descriptive subordinate clause:

The Hindenburg – gigantic and imposing – *had taken five years to build.*

4. Then and now

Like the first technique, this method presents two opposing attitudes. This time, however, the first comes from before the focal event of the explanation, and the second from after it, hinting at how that event has changed the world. This second perspective may be made explicit or left implicit.

In Roman times *people thought that the slopes of Vesuvius were a relatively safe place to live.* **Now** *we know that Vesuvius is a dangerous and active volcano.*

5. ...little did they know

This approach uses dual perspectives to establish a common idea or attitude prior to the focal event. A contrasting, unforeseen outcome is then introduced with an ellipsis and 'little did they know':

*Passengers on board the Titanic thought her unsinkable**... little did they know they would soon be facing disaster.***

Structural model part 4: What happens /How it works or What happened and why

Again, the contents of this part of the text vary dramatically across the three explanation sub-genres. Therefore, they will be covered in their own separate sections.

Structural model part 4: What happens

For: Explanation of a process

This section provides a sequential explanation of the focal process, organised into the stages that were detailed in the previous structural section. Each stage forms a separate paragraph.

Language features:

1. Subheadings

Begin each new stage with an appropriate subheading that links clearly and succinctly to the labels provided in the previous structural section (number for clarity if necessary):

Stage 1: The Egg.
Stage 2: The Tadpole.
Stage 3: The Adult Frog.

(Life cycle of a frog)

Or

Phase 1: Evaporation.
Phase 2: Condensation.
Phase 3: Precipitation.
Phase 4: Infiltration.

(Water cycle)

Or

Step 1: Sorting.
Step 2: Collection.
Step 3: Processing.
Step 4: Re-purposing.

(Recycling)

2. Sequence words

Due to the step-by-step nature of a process, sequential openers are a key feature of this structural element. They are particularly useful as paragraph starters if sub-headings are not numbered:

First, *the bear eats and drinks excessively to prepare for hibernation.*

Next, *they reduce their eating but continue to drink to purge waste.*

After that, *the bears hibernate and their heart rate drops to 8-21 bpm.*

As a result, *their blood flow reduces by up to 45 per cent.*

Consequently, *they can be slow to rise and run in the winter.*

Finally, *the bears wake and their metabolic rate adjusts to summer levels.*

3. Noun, who/which/where,

A two-part sentence that describes the key event of the stage while providing extra information about a component part in the form of a subordinate clause:

The water, which is being heated by the sun, *begins to evaporate.*

The heart, where the soul was believed to reside, *was left intact.*

The cement, which will hold the bricks in place, *is left to set for 24 hours.*

4. Conditionals

Some parts of the process may depend on the outcome of others. This can be demonstrated using conditionals, using 'if', 'then', etc:

If the water freezes, **then** it will have to thaw before evaporation can take place.

If the water runs off the surface, **then** it joins a larger water source.

If the clouds become heavy with rain, **then** precipitation takes place.

5. Verb and verb

This approach presents two actions (often interdependent or consequential) in one sentence:

The water vapour **cools and condenses** *to form clouds.*

The tadpole **escapes and swims** *from the egg.*

The bear **eats and drinks** *to prepare for hibernation.*

6. Adverb,

By placing the adverb of manner first, this technique accentuates **how** the stage is carried out:

Slowly, the tadpole emerges from the egg.

Carefully, the bricks are put in place.

Eventually, the water filters through the rock.

7. BOYS

BOYS is an acronym where each letter stands for a useful connective, reminding writers to link their ideas:

But   *The tadpole is twice as big, **but** still has a tail.*

Or   *The water might infiltrate the ground **or** run off the surface.*

Yet   *The nutrients are removed, **yet** the mass retains water.*

So   *The water is absorbed, **so** the waste is ready to expel.*

8. Description: reason

This technique is a concise way of presenting information for both cause and effect:

The clouds become heavy: they are full of water.

The bear is drowsy: its metabolism is still very slow.

The teeth are clean: the brush has removed the plaque.

9. Name (aka)

The abbreviation 'aka' (also known as) can be used to introduce technical language in an accessible, supportive way:

*The heating process **(aka evaporation)** can happen very quickly.*

*The build-up of debris on the teeth **(aka plaque)** is removed by the brush.*

*The eggs **(aka spawn)** soon hatch.*

10. When; when; when, then

This is a useful technique for concluding the final paragraph of the main explanation, as it provides the reader with a process checklist, as well as an expected final outcome:

When the tail has disappeared; *when* it has grown front and back legs; *when* it emerges onto land, *then* the frog has reached maturity.

Structural model part 4: How it works

For: How things work

This structural element comprises of an explanation of how the parts of the focal subject function together to achieve an outcome. It is usually organised into sequential stages, already identified in the previous section of the explanation. Each function forms a separate paragraph.

Language features:

1. Subheadings

Each separate function should be introduced via an appropriate subheading that links to the stages identified in the previous section. This can be structured in one of two main ways:

Number then heading:

Stage 1: Sorting.

Stage 1: Mastication.

Stage 1: Inhalation.

… or heading alone. (The subsequent paragraph then opens with a sequential connective):

Sorting
First, the rubbish is sorted, depending on what it is made of.

Mastication
First, the food is broken up by the molars and saliva is added.

Inhalation
First, air is taken into the lungs via the mouth and nose.

2. Sequence word,

Following on from the initial opener, sequential openers are again a key feature of this part of the text:

Firstly, *the food is broken up by the molars and saliva is added.*

Next, *the softened food travels down the oesophagus to the stomach.*

After that, *acid is added to break down the food further.*

As a result, *the nutrients are more easily removed in the small intestine.*

Consequently, *the water is removed in the large intestine.*

Finally, *the waste is excreted.*

3. Noun, who/which/where,

A two-part sentence which includes extra descriptive information in a subordinate clause:

*The filament, **which heats to 100 $^{\circ}$C,** boils the water.*

*The small intestine, **which can measure about seven metres in length,** extracts the nutrients from the food.*

*The heart, **which has two atria and two ventricles,** pumps the oxygen-rich blood around the body.*

4. Must consequences

This technique is useful for showing the interrelated nature of some processes. It highlights critical, dependent relationships using the word 'must':

*For the water to boil, the temperature **must** reach 100°C.*

*For the eye to work, light **must** be present.*

*For the food to be broken down, acid **must** be added in the stomach.*

5. _____ , which

A two-part sentence which is useful for conveying extra information, particularly when applied to a cause-and-effect process:

*The pupil opens wide, **which** lets more light in.*

*The teeth grind the food, **which** breaks it into small pieces.*

*The Earth rotates on its axis, **which** takes approximately 24 hours.*

6. Verb and verb

This method presents two interdependent or consequential actions in one sentence:

*The fuel **ignites and burns** to produce energy.*

*The rubbish is **sorted and collected** by refuse technicians.*

*The muscles **expand and contract** to move the food through.*

7. Needs: reason

A variation on the cause-and-effect structure that is often seen in explanation texts, this technique accentuates the **necessity** of the focal aspect:

*An engine **needs** petrol: **this is the fuel that burns to create power.***

*Muscles **need** oxygen: **it is used to generate movement energy.***

*A kettle **needs** electricity: **it cannot heat water without it.***

8. BOYS

BOYS is an acronym where each letter stands for a useful connective, reminding writers to link their ideas:

But	*The intestine extracts vitamins, **but** also extracts fat.*
Or	*The heart can process oxygen rich **or** oxygen poor blood.*
Yet	*We do burn some fat during the day, **yet** dedicated exercise is crucial.*
So	*The water is absorbed, **so** the waste is ready to expel.*

9. Reference to diagrams

The author may engage the reader by including a visual aid, such as a diagram of the working subject, then reference this diagram as part of the explanation:

(Note: this method is also useful in explanations of processes, which may contain flow charts or cycle diagrams.)

***As you can see from the diagram,** the heart has four valves.*

***As you can see from the diagram,** the filament is at the bottom of the kettle.*

***As you can see from the diagram,** the oesophagus connects the mouth to the stomach.*

10. Once and now

This method is useful for the final stage of the explanatory section, as it compares how something **started** with how it **ends**:

Once *discarded waste, the recycled material is* **now** *ready to be re-used.*

Once *a healthy treat, this food is* **now** *devoid of nutrients and water.*

Once *a fossil fuel, the petrol has* **now** *been burned to create kinetic energy.*

Structural model part 4: What happened and why

For: Why something happened

In this particular sub-genre, the main explanatory section is usually 'cause-and-effect' based, with key points and reasons combined and elaborated upon in **paragraphs**, rather than through a sequential process description.

Language features:

I. Subheadings
(Note: At times subheadings may interrupt the flow of the text for this explanation type. Only use when appropriate.)

Rather than merely serving a practical, informative function, subheadings in this sub-genre can be more dramatic, and thus more engaging. This can be organised in one of two ways:

Number then heading:

Stage 1: The Warning.

Stage 2: The Iceberg.

Stage 3: The Impact.

Stage 4: The Aftermath.

...or heading alone. The subsequent paragraph opens with a sequential connective:

The Warning
Firstly, *the ship received a radio warning, but...*

The Iceberg
Secondly, *spotters on the ship noticed the iceberg, however...*

The Impact
Thirdly, *the ship slammed into the iceberg, which...*

The Aftermath
Finally, *the ship began to break up, causing...*

(Note: Beyond 'thirdly', encourage the use of alternative sequential connectives.)

2. Dates, times and places

If not already established in the introductory sections of the explanation, dates, times and locations will be critical elements in the explanation of an event:

On May 3rd 1937, in Frankfurt, Germany, *97 people departed aboard the Hindenburg.*

On the 28th January 1986, *seven astronauts boarded the Challenger spaceship at* **Cape Canaveral.**

Amelia Earhart disappeared on **July 2nd, 1937, somewhere over the Pacific Ocean.**

3. Facts and figures

In this text type, it is of critical importance to include subject-specific information in a concise manner:

The Hindenburg was carrying **97 people,** *of whom* **36 were passengers** *and* **61 were crewmen.**

Between **1981 and 1986,** *more than* **twenty Space Transportation Systems** *had been launched successfully from* **Cape Canaveral.**

Amelia Earhart's intended destination was called **Howland Island**, *which measured*

2,000 metres long and *500 metres wide.*

4. Noun, who/which/where,

This techniques helps to convey detailed additional information within a subordinate clause:

The cellars under Parliament, **where the gunpowder was kept,** *were damp and dark.*

Fawkes' stepfather, **who was a recusant Catholic,** *inspired him to fight for his faith.*

King James I, **who was due to open Parliament the next day,** *ordered a search.*

5. Reasons and results

These are two separate techniques which use key words to demonstrate the critical cause-and-effect element of an explanation. Both work well as paragraph openers:

Reason:

The main reason *for the Wall Street crash was…*

Another reason *for the economic downturn was…*

A further reason *is…*

Result:

As a result of *mass migration from rural areas, the American farming industry suffered, which meant that…*

Production declined, construction was sluggish, debt was high, and **as a result,** *the market crashed.*

6. BOYS

BOYS is an acronym where each letter stands for a useful connective, reminding writers to link their ideas:

But   *The ship received warnings, **but** they were ignored.*

Or   *It is unknown whether the city faced a catastrophe, **or** simply became less and less inhabited with the passage of time.*

Yet   *The wind was high, **yet** the aircraft took off.*

So   *The vessel began to sink, **so** the travellers abandoned ship.*

7. As sentences

This sentence type replaces 'because' with 'as'. It varies the vocabulary of cause-and-effect statements:

*The hydrogen was dangerous **as** it could ignite easily.*

*The transmission was important **as** the whole world was listening.*

*The gunpowder rotted **as** the cellars were too damp.*

8. Some / Many sentences

This technique allows the writer to demonstrate how groups of various sizes contributed to, or reacted to, the event being explained:

***Some** people continued their frivolous spending, despite the warnings.*

***Some** people leapt off the sinking ship into the icy waters.*

***Many** people scrambled to the lifeboats as soon as the alarm was raised.*

***Many** people were put to death for faith-based crimes, which angered religious groups.*

This technique could also be used with the term 'whilst' to draw a comparison between different reactions:

Many *people scrambled to the lifeboats as soon as the alarm was raised,* **whilst some** *people leapt off the sinking ship into the icy waters.*

9. 3 action starter sentences

Considering the linear narrative approach often adopted in this sub-genre, this final technique aims to engage the reader in the explanation through the description of exciting, linked actions:

Alarms sounded, lights flashed, people screamed: yet escape was impossible.

Crowds cheered, flags fluttered, tears fell: man had landed on the Moon.

Stocks plummeted, businesses failed, people lamented: the Great Depression had begun.

Structural model 5: What happened next or something interesting

This final, summative section concludes the explanation by situating the results in context and/or providing the reader with some final detail that will interest them.

Language features:

I. Most important – in short
For: Explanation of a process / How things work / Why something happened

This technique reiterates the key points or events of the explanation, then sums them up in one succinct statement:

After a time the frog will have completed all its changes and will be ready to start breeding *– in short,* *the cycle will begin again.*

After the pupil has allowed light to pass to the retina and through the optic nerve, the brain receives, inverts and processes the image *– in short,* *the parts of the eye work together to allow us to see.*

The ship was ill-equipped, overloaded, and multiple warnings were ignored *– in short,* *the Titanic was a disaster waiting to happen.*

2. Noun, who/which/where, summary/facts
For: Explanation of a process / How things work / Why something happened

This technique delivers summative information or additional interesting facts:

(Note: overuse of **any** of these techniques negates impact. Although they are applicable in a number of structural sections, pupils should be encouraged to use each technique for effect, with a possible ceiling of two or three times per text.)

The cycle, **which has included two changes of state,** *will continue to repeat over and over.*

The postal system, **which processes more than 68 million letters a day,** *includes more than 12,000 post offices.*

The Black Death, **which killed more than a third over the world's population,** *is still considered the most deadly disease outbreak in history.*

3. Complete: details
For: Explanation of a process

This closing technique informs the reader that the process is complete, then details the expected result/outcome:

The process is complete: the frog has reached maturity and may breed in order to begin the cycle again.

The process is complete: the recycled material is ready to be used in a new product.

The process is complete: the mummified body is ready to be placed in the tomb.

4. Did you know?
For: How things work

This method engages the reader with an interesting fact presented in the form of a rhetorical question:

Did you know... *more than 205 million engines are produced in the UK every year?*

Did you know... *a mouse's heart beats about 500 times per minute?*

Did you know... *if you liquidised the Earth and poured it into a container the size of the Sun, it would take 1,300,000 Earths to fill it?*

5. Then and now
For: Why something happened

This closing technique explains how the perspectives and/or knowledge of those involved was modified in the light of the focal event:

In 1912 people thought the Titanic unsinkable. **Now** *we know that even man's most formidable structures are at risk when Mother Nature strikes.*

In 1929 people failed to predict the coming financial crisis. **Now** *we see clearly just how damaging irresponsible bankers can be.*

In 1605 people thought Parliament was safe and secure. **Now** *we know just how close it came to being destroyed.*

6. What + ! authorial opinion
For: Explanation of a process / How things work / Why something happened

This technique gives the explanation a more informal tone. It expresses surprise, satisfaction and/or appreciation of the outcome. It may be particularly suited to younger audiences:

What *an extraordinary journey the caterpillar has taken*!

What *an amazing feat of engineering*!

What *an historic, memorable event*!

7. Fact, therefore
For: Explanation of a process / How things work / Why something happened

This method is useful when the writer wishes to include some lasting message or influence:

The lifecycle is a very delicate process. Therefore, *we should do our best to help conserve the habitats of these animals.*

The process of building engines can be costly and can damage the environment. Therefore, *we hope that scientists continue to research new, cheaper, more ecologically friendly sources of energy.*

The Hindenburg disaster was a tragic loss of life that should never have happened. Therefore, *mass transit vehicles must now go through rigorous safety checks.*

7. Extra information
For: Explanation of a process / How things work / Why something happened

Better than simply providing extra information at the end of the explanation, this techniques encourages the reader to seek out these facts themselves by providing appropriate (and, wherever possible, genuine!) sources of information:

Visit www.frogsjourney.com *to discover more about the lifecycle of a frog.*

Check out www.howitworks.com *for more fascinating explanations.*

Continue your research at *www.titanicwreckage.com.*

The Hindenburg Disaster: Why it Happened

Completed in 1936 by The Zeppelin Company (aka Luftschiffbau Zeppelin GmbH), the Hindenburg was a large, luxurious airship. In fact, the LZ 129 Hindenburg, which was its official title, was the largest object to have ever flown. The question is: what caused the tragic destruction of this amazing feat of engineering?

The Hindenburg – vast and imposing – took five years to build. Its construction took place on the shores of Lake Constance, in the university city of Friedrichshafen, Germany. The dimensions of the airship were staggering: it measured 245 metres in length and had a diameter of more than 40 metres. At maximum capacity, it could hold 133 people (61 crew members and 72 passengers). Initially, helium was chosen as the lifting gas, as it was not flammable, and therefore considered to be safer. However, with the gas in short supply, the designers were forced to use hydrogen instead. At the time, this was still thought to be a safe option. Now we know that it was a major factor in the disaster.

The First Flights
Five years after its construction began in 1931, the maiden test flight of the Hindenburg took place on March 4th, 1936. The airship left the Zeppelin dockyards with 87 people on board, including 30 dockyard employees who were flying as passengers. The airship would go on to complete six more trial flights before being put into commercial use, where it would fly safely and successfully for 14 months. Considering this, as well as the previous German history of flying hydrogen-filled passenger airships without injury or fatality, many believed that German engineers had fully mastered the safe use of hydrogen. Little did they know, they would soon witness a terrible tragedy.

The Disaster
On May 3rd 1937, in Frankfurt, Germany, 97 people boarded the Hindenburg (of whom 36 were passengers and 61 were crewmen). As the airship approached its destination of the Lakehurst Naval Air Station in New Jersey, America, it prepared for a 'flying moor' landing. This meant that long ropes would be dropped from the ship, so that they could be tied on and the ship winched in from below. The weather worsened, and the captain was struggling to position the ship correctly when, all of a sudden, the Hindenburg caught fire. Witnesses screamed, coughed and ran for cover as the Hindenburg fell, smoking and flaming, from the sky. The entire ship was engulfed in flames in less than a minute: some people put the time at as little as 16 seconds. Amazingly, despite the enormous inferno, 62 people out of the 97 on board survived.

The Theories
Many scientists, engineers and others have put forward explanations for the Hindenburg disaster. Some people have suggested that the ship was struck by lightning, which ignited the hydrogen gas being vented while the ship was making its descent. Some blamed a static spark, which was caused by a build-up of static electricity. Another potential explanation was that an engine had backfired during a hard turn, sending out sparks which started the blaze. The hydrogen used as a lifting gas, a punctured gas cell, and even the paint on the ship, have all been blamed at some time or another by various people for starting the blaze. There was even talk, at the time, of sabotage, with Hugo Eckener (former head of the Zeppelin Company) suggesting that someone could have shot the airship out of the sky.

To this day, there is still no proven explanation for the Hindenburg disaster. The accident, which received global news coverage, destroyed public confidence in the giant airship. Therefore, the airship era drew to a sad end. The site of the Hindenburg crash is now marked by a chain-fenced pad and a memorial with a bronze plaque where the airship's gondola landed. The memorial was dedicated on the 50th anniversary of the disaster, on May 6, 1987.

Continue your research at www.airships.net/hindenburg

REPORT WRITING

DEFINITION: A report is a fact-based account written about a broad range of natural, cultural or social phenomena, often undertaken as the result of an investigation and/or research. It provides a written account (though reports can also be oral) of something a pupil has done, observed or thoroughly researched.

PURPOSE: All reports are written to inform, though some can be written to demonstrate the depth of understanding and level of research undertaken by the writer - such reports are often part of the formal exam system. Other reports are written to persuade (using a wealth of factual evidence to make or support a point).

AUDIENCE: The audience for a report is usually known, and in all cases a report must communicate information accurately and succinctly to the target audience. Reports are essentially formal, though there should be some adaptation of language and content in relation to the target audience (e.g. if the target audience are experts, then the writing will differ to that of a report written for an audience with no prior knowledge of the subject).

SUGGESTED STIMULI & RELATED ACTIVITIES

Stimuli for report writing are innumerable: a report can be written on any theme or idea which demands research on the part of the writer. Useful categories of stimuli include:

1. Interest-driven stimuli

As reports are the direct result of 'finding out' (research) then a subject which the pupils generate themselves will undoubtedly result in a far more engaging report.

Teachers who are particularly keen to explore the benefits of interest-driven learning should read the work of Mihaly Csikszentmihalyi. One of the key findings of his research is the fact that interest is related to both quality of experience as well as achievement. Staff wishing to find out more should begin by looking at the concept of *affective* states.

2. 'Working question' stimuli.

The working question is the query that the writer seeks to 'answer' through the report. It is used as a point of reference against which to assess the relevance of information. Exam questions often take this form and it is, therefore, a question type which should be explicitly discussed with pupils:

What impact did Ghandi's ideas and actions have on the Indian independence movement?

What was Nelson Mandela's key achievement?

It is also productive to discuss how **not** to answer this kind of 'working question'. The worst way to answer either of these working questions would be to report everything they (the pupil) know about the subject, without considering **relevance**. It is essential that pupils are taught how to unpick the **key words** (e.g. 'impact' and 'achievement' in the examples above) from these types of questions.

3. Describe the impact of...

'Impact Reports' are essentially a persuasive form of report. Importantly, the key method used to persuade the reader is the accumulation of a wealth of facts (often combined with quotes from experts and statistical data).

Examples:

What impact has global warming had in the last century?
(Starting with a question)

The impact of global warming in the last century.
(Starting with a statement which becomes the title of the report)

4. Named subjects

Often the title of a report is merely a naming of the subject e.g.

Examples:

Spiders.
The Impressionists.
London.

This kind of report allows the pupil to demonstrate the breadth of their research.

5. Analytical reports

The title of these reports often opens with the word 'How'. For example,

How the school football team performed this year.

How our school can become even more exciting.

They include an element of explanation, but importantly they report about the **current situation** (facts, data etc.) and conclude with an analytical summary which can also suggest ways to progress (i.e. how the football team might improve next year based on an analysis of what they have done this year).

STRUCTURAL MODEL

Effective reports have a logical flow of ideas and are structurally cohesive. Although reports are highly structured, there is **no single correct structural model**. However, when teaching report writing in the primary sector, it is wise to provide one simple structural model to begin with (so that pupils can concentrate on 'composition and effect'). Once pupils are familiar with this model, other reports can be analysed structurally so that pupils gradually become aware of the wide variety of structural models.

The following models are 'tried and tested', and are simple without being reductive. They are also easy to remember!

STRUCTURAL MODEL 1: 3 TELLS

Pupil 'access' language	Meta language	Structural Model part (teacher use)
1. Tell the reader what you're about to tell them	1.Introductory summary of what is to follow	1. Opening
2. Tell them in detail	2. Main body content	2. Main content
3. Tell them the key points again and explain WHY you told them	3. Summary and significance	3. Closing

The second element of the '3 Tells' model (the content of the main body of the report) can take many different forms, but must **always** be **logically organised**.

Ways of logically organising the main body ('tell them in detail') include:

- Key points with the most important first: a useful way of drawing the reader in with something significant.
- Key points with the most important last: this leaves a key point lingering in the reader's mind.
- Cause and effect.
- Alphabetic: only use this organisation device if **all** of the key points are of equal significance.

STRUCTURAL MODEL 2: THE W'S MODEL

An alternative model to '3 Tells', the W's structural model is once again (deliberately) easy to remember, and works well when writing simple factual reports about a given subject (other than a report about a famous person):

Pupil 'access' language	Meta language	Structural Model part (teacher use)
1. What they are AND what they belong to	1. Classification statement	1. Opening
2. What they look like	2. Appearance	2. Main content
3. Where you find them	3. Location	
4. What they do	4. Function	
5. Why they are important	5. Significance/purpose	3. Closing
6. Wow!	6. Something of particular interest and/or significance	

Note: In both models a 'structural model part' column has been included. This is so that you can link the writing techniques that follow with the appropriate structural element, regardless of which model you choose.

Structural model part 1: Opening

The opening of any report should be a description of the key points of the main body of the report in condensed form. It is also known as a 'digest' and sometimes an 'abstract'. It should be direct and concise.

Language features:

1. Classification

Applicable to a range of topics and structures, but particularly useful if using the W's structural model. The opening may include a classification/ 'belonging to' statement, using key linking words to identify the subject as part of a group:

Spiders belong to the arachnid family.

The Titanic was a ship of the White Star line.

The playwright William Shakespeare is one of the most revered authors in the English canon.

2. Noun, who/which/where,

This concise and versatile technique can be used anywhere in a report, but it is particularly well suited to the opening section, as it allows for a fact-rich 'double shot' of information to be conveyed in a single sentence via the inclusion of a subordinate clause. It starts with a noun, continuing with additional information presented as a subordinate clause (between commas, brackets, or dashes) and ends with the continuation of the main clause:

Queen Victoria, who was England's longest serving monarch, came to the throne on the 20th June, 1837.

Marvel Comics, which was originally called 'Timely Comics', is the biggest producer of comic books in the world.

The Bermuda Triangle, where some travellers are still scared to go, is a mysterious area in the North Atlantic Ocean.

3. BOYS

BOYS stands for 'But', 'Or', 'Yet' and 'So'. It is an acronymic reminder of useful connectives which could again be employed in sentences in any part of a report, but suits the opening well as it enables the writer to convey ample information in one sentence:

There are many species of venomous snake in the world, yet the inland taipan snake has the most deadly venom of all.

The Chicago Bulls were a very successful basketball team in the 90s, but one player stands out above all: Michael Jordan.

The Apollo missions are considered one of Man's greatest triumphs, yet they began with the tragedy of Apollo 1.

4. De: de

De: de is an associative label which stands for 'Description: details'. Again, it is well suited to report writing, and particularly to the opening section, as it is a fact-rich sentence type which opens with a description of the subject, then expands on that description (after a colon) with additional details in a subordinate clause:

The Moon was formed 4.6 billion years ago: it is Earth's only natural satellite

The Amazon rainforest is the largest tropical rainforest in the world: it covers more than five and a half a million square kilometres.

The skin is the largest organ in the human body: on average it has a surface areas of about two square metres.

5. The question is: ?

This final opening technique is useful as it creates a bridge between the introductory section of the report and the main body content. It is actually a two-sentence structure; the first presents a fact about the subject, and the second uses a rhetorical question (based on the preceding fact) to intrigue the reader and encourage them to read on:

King Henry VIII was a powerful, revered leader. The question is: what led to his demise?

The Black Death was a terrible disease that killed millions. The question is: how did it spread?

The Victorian era was a time of great prosperity in Britain. The question is: what led to this financial shift?

Structural model part 2: Main content

Reports fall mainly into three categories: descriptive, analytical and evaluative (sometimes they combine one or more of these categories). In all instances, especially in the main body, the writing should be objective and fact-rich.

Effective reports are impersonal – consistent use of the third person and passive voice should be modelled and discussed. Although the **impact** of a report (about famine, a natural catastrophe etc.) may cause an emotional response in the reader, the **content** of the report should be impartial. Reports should inform or persuade with the wealth of their factual content, and not with emotive language.

Please note that the content suggestions and language features which make up the main body of the report are dependent on the subject of the report. The following suggestions will **not** all be appropriate for every report. For this reason, it is essential that pupils grasp the necessity of selecting **pertinent** language features for the subject of their report. Those listed below therefore function as a menu-of-possibilities rather than a sequential list of prerequisites.

Sentence types 2, 3 and 4 from Structural model part I are also appropriate for use in the main body content.

Language features:

1. The W's

Just as in journalistic reporting, answering the W's is an important key element of the main body of a written report. Note, however, that it is not 'All the W's'. Pupils should only address those which clearly relate to the subject of their report. This is a skill which should be modelled and explicitly discussed. Briefly, the W's are...

Who they are / **What** it is:

The octopus is a cephalopod mollusc with eight arms, no bones and a hard beak.

What it / they do:

Open-ocean octopuses usually inject their prey with a paralysing saliva before tearing it to pieces with their beaks.

Why it does it / they do it:

Most octopuses are able to eject thick, dark ink in a large cloud to help them escape from predators.

Where it is from / they are from:

Octopuses live in many different regions of the ocean, including pelagic (open) waters, coral reefs, and on the ocean floor.

When it happened / they did it:

The first identifiable octopus species began to appear approximately 500 million years ago.

Why it/they are important:

In many parts of the world, humans eat octopus. Depending on species and location, the arms and sometimes other parts of the body are prepared in different ways.

2. The BIG 'E'

...and that is **evidence**. The easiest way to teach this is to explain to pupils that when they state a **fact**, they should then state how they **know** it's a fact. This can take many forms, such as quotes from experts or book references. It may be useful to produce a poster of useful sentence starters which include the keyword 'fact', such as:

The first fact to consider...
A further fact...
According to experts, the fact that...
A well-known fact about...
Additional facts...
...etc.

A further fact, which was explained by the ancient Greek philosopher Anaxagoras (d. 428 B.C.), is that the Moon does not produce its own light, but reflects the light of the Sun.

According to historical experts, the fact that Tutankhamun's skull showed signs of impact damage supports the notion that he was murdered.

A well-known fact about bats is that they use echolocation to help them hunt in the dark.

3. Up - to - dates

An 'up-to-date' is any sentence or paragraph which demonstrates that the information included in the report is both recent and relevant. To that end, they must include at least the month and year, if not the full date:

A study published in October 2013 suggests that the world polar bear population is still in decline.

- (as a sentence for a report written in December 2013)

Tests carried out in March this year show that around 30 per cent of children in the UK are overweight or obese.

- (as a sentence for a report written that year - implied)

An investigation undertaken in July 2013 revealed that more than 2,000 different species of butterflies live in the rainforests of South America.

- (as a sentence for a report written in September 2013)

4. Number sentences

Statistical data is a key element of many reports (particularly those which aim to persuade). These can take the form of simple numbers, or could be percentages and/or fractions:

There are eight planets in the Solar System and Earth is the third closest to the Sun.

- Simple numbers

There are more than 470 different species of shark, including the apex-predator Great White, which can grow up to 8m (26ft long) and weigh up to 3,324 kg (7,328 lb).

- More complex numbers

In 2009 there were more than 310 million people in the United States, with males accounting for just under half (49%) of the population.

- Percentages and fractions

5. 2A/4A sentences

The name of this simple sentence type does not relate to writing levels, but rather stands for '2 Adjectives' or '4 Adjectives'. It reminds pupils to expand descriptions using an adjective list, separated by a comma. This sentence type suits report writing, as it increases descriptive detail whilst helping to maintain the flow of writing:

- 2A (Two adjectives before a noun)

*The crocodile is a **well-adapted, patient** hunter.*

*The Hindenburg was a **colossal, ambitious** design.*

*Football is a **team-based, global** sport.*

- 4A (Two adjectives before a first noun, followed by two adjectives before a second noun)

*Comics are an **accessible, entertaining** medium with a **long, rich** history.*

*Twitter is a **popular, web-based** network used by a **large, diverse** group of people.*

*Bananas are **curved, elongated** fruits which grow mainly in **warm, sunny** climates.*

6. No contractions

This is an aspect of formal written language. Contractions are often used to mirror speech, or to create a personal, casual tone. As such, it is a useful exercise (and will aid pupils' understanding of apostrophe usage) to convert contractions to their expanded form and back again, at word level, then at sentence level, using existing reports as stimuli:

It's – It is
Couldn't – Could not
That's – That is
Should've – Should have
Can't – Cannot
They're – They are

*Pufferfish can breathe underwater: **they're** equipped with gills. (NO)*
*Pufferfish can breathe underwater: **they are** equipped with gills. (YES)*

*Tutankhamun **could've** died from a horse-riding accident, but scientists **can't** tell for certain. (NO)*
*Tutankhamun **could have** died from a horse-riding accident, but scientists **cannot** tell for certain. (YES)*

*Humans **can't** see in the dark, as the eyeball needs light to work. (NO)*
*Humans **cannot** see in the dark, as the eyeball needs light to work. (YES)*

7. Phrase lists

Although list sentences are overused in many genres, particularly narrative, in the context of report writing they are a useful vehicle for delivering a wealth of facts succinctly. In a standard list sentence, single words are separated with commas, but in a phrase list semi-colons are more often used:

Spiders have eight legs; between two and twelve eyes; delicate bodies and often have hair.

Henry VIII had six wives: he divorced two, beheaded two, one died after childbirth and one survived after he passed away.

There are four types of tissues in the human body: epithelial which protects against moisture loss; connective which provides structure, nervous which coordinates activity and muscle which contracts.

8. Name – adjective pair –

Once pupils are familiar with using adjective lists to describe the subject of their report (see pages 93 and 94), this technique allows them to manipulate the structure of their descriptions further, thus demonstrating writing proficiency through use of a variety of sentence types. Here, the adjectives are presented in a pair as a subordinate clause, marked with dashes. One effective way to teach this is to provide a simple descriptive sentence:

Rhinos are impressive creatures.

…and ask pupils for two adjectives that describe the subject (e.g. 'large' and 'powerful'). Then demonstrate how these can be integrated into the sentence as a subordinate clause using dashes:

*Rhinos – **large and powerful** – are impressive creatures.*

Another effective method of teaching this technique is to start with a '2A' sentence (See page 93) and show how it can be changed into a 'Name – adjective pair –' by altering the order and adding an extra adjective:

*The Hindenburg was a **colossal, ambitious** design.*
becomes
*The Hindenburg – **colossal and ambitious** – was an **impressive** design.*

*The crocodile is a **well-adapted, patient** hunter.*
becomes
*The crocodile – **well-adapted and patient** – is an **effective** hunter.*

9. Verb to noun sentences

These are quite difficult to grasp initially and serve as a higher-order language feature of report writing. The technical term is **nominalisation**, and it involves using a verb, an adjective, or an adverb as the head of a noun phrase. The technique is best explained by example:

We **run** to raise money for Water Aid.
   verb

becomes

The **run** raised money for Water Aid.
verb turned into noun form

Effective writers may **edit** *their work for hours*
An **edit** *may take hours for an effective writer.*

Octopuses usually **react** *to threats by squirting ink and hiding.*
A threatened Octopus' **reaction** *is usually to squirt ink and hide.*

10. Here and there / this and that sentences

Even in a report about a single subject, the technique of contrasting will shed light on the specific focus of the report, as this sentence type demonstrates:

The English spiders studied in this report are harmless, but in other countries, such as Australia, there are spiders which can harm and even kill people.

The country of France, which is studied in this report, has a population of almost 66 million people. By contrast, its neighbour Germany has a population of about 80 million.

Superman has the ability to fly; see through walls; lift whole planets and emit heat energy from his eyes, yet many other superheroes only have one superpower.

11. Tell: show 3; sentences

This sentence structure, often used in narrative writing, also suits the fact-rich, informative aims of report writing. The sentence opens with a main clause containing a fact about the subject, then continues with a subordinate clause in the form of a phrase list, containing three different pieces of evidence. In other words, the first part 'tells' the reader the fact, and the second part 'shows' them the evidence:

The digestive system is a complex mechanism: breaking down food; removing and absorbing nutrients; expelling waste matter.

Sharks are skilled hunters: they have a keen sense of smell; they can swim at high speeds; they are armed with row upon row of razor-sharp teeth.

Plants are key to human survival: they provide us with food; they clean the air we breathe; they even give us building and writing materials.

This sentence type could also be presented using **bullet points**, another key feature of report writing:

The digestive system is a complex mechanism:
- *It breaks down food.*
- *It removes and absorbs nutrients.*
- *It expels waste matter.*

12. Visuals

Most reports use visuals to support the written statements. These might include:

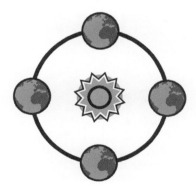

Diagrams

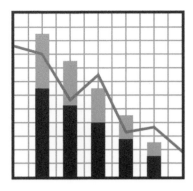

Graphs

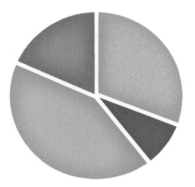

Pie charts

A Great White Shark

Captioned photographs

It is important to discuss the necessary data labels and titles that should be included with these visuals, providing a useful cross-curricular link with maths and computing. Pupils can collect their own data and create appropriately labelled charts as supportive visuals, integrating their findings into the report.

13. Brackets and asterisks

At times, technical language may be needed in report writing. If this is the case, then a simple bracketed description of the technical word or phrase is added on the first occasion that it is used (but not thereafter):

*Blood contains three different types of cells: red blood cells; white blood cells; and platelets **(cells that help to stop the organism from bleeding).***

*Kangaroos carry their developing young in a marsupium **(pouch)** for at least 190 days.*

As a higher-level writing skill, you may want to introduce the idea of using the asterisk*. This is placed after the technical term, then a linked explanation is provided at the bottom of the page (or in a glossary for an extended piece):

Felix Kelly's painting included a number of recurring motifs, such as red and white striped deckchairs.*

*a decorative design that is repeated

Structural model part 3: Closing

By this point in a report (if it is an effective example) the reader will have been provided with a broad body of relevant information. At the end of the report, they should be succinctly reminded of the key points.

Language features:

The key to an effective report conclusion is the **2 S's:**

Summary and **Significance**

1. Summary sentences

These aid the reader by repeating and emphasising the main points of the report in more general terms. It is therefore necessary to vary the vocabulary from that previously used in the explanations in the main body of the report. Useful sentence starters for the summary might be provided to help:

In short...
In conclusion...
To sum up...
The point of...

In conclusion, the Hindenburg was an ambitious yet doomed project, mainly due to the lack of safety precautions taken during its maiden voyage.

To sum up, although the great white shark is an effective predator, it is less dangerous to humans than snakes, wasps and even bees!

In short, the manner in which the youngest pharaoh died is still debated: some evidence points to an accidental death; some points to murder.

2. Significance sentences

'Significance' refers to a major point, either repeated from earlier in the report using different language **or** introduced for the first time for effect (we remember final points!):

*Although the average mosquito measures less than 1.5cm and has a lifespan of less than a month, **they are considered the most dangerous animals on the planet, killing 725,000 people a year with the diseases carried in their*** *blood.*

*The rainforest, with its rich variety of wildlife and its majestic canopies filled with many different plant species, is a fascinating topic. However, **an area of a rainforest the size of a football field is being destroyed every second of every day.***

*Our solar system is vast, and the measurements involved are extraordinary. However, if you consider that the diameter of our sun is 1,391,684 km, **while the diameter of one of the largest known stars, VY Canis Majoris, is 1,975,000,000 km (about 1400 times bigger) the relative enormity of space is immediately evident.***

THE MEGALODON

Today, sharks have a reputation for being vicious, efficient killing machines, but about ten million years ago there lived a shark that would make even the largest and fiercest great white swim for cover: the megalodon. This extinct giant of the sea, whose name means 'big tooth' in ancient Greek, lived 15.9 to 2.6 million years ago, in the Cenozoic Era*. In some literature, it is classified as 'Carcharodon megalodon', yet others have classified it as 'Carcharocles megalodon'. Either way, it was a vast, powerful predator that ruled the seas. The question is: what exactly made this carnivore so very dangerous?

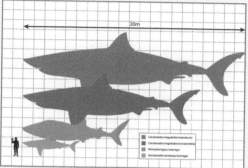

The megalodon – fierce and deadly – has been compared with the great white shark (Carcharodon carcharias) in terms of its looks: it has a slender, streamlined shape and is armed with a large mouth full of sharp, serrated teeth. However, while great white sharks grow to a maximum of about 8 metres, the megalodon could grow to a whopping 20 metres, about two and-a-half times as long! Their triangular teeth made for devastating weapons: they measured more than 10cm each in height, had serrated edges, and they were perpetually replaced throughout the megalodon's life.

Considering the fact that seas were much warmer at the time when megalodon lived, this powerful predator could be found in oceans all around the world. They could also live in a range of marine environments: shallow coastal waters; swampy coastal lagoons; offshore deep water environments and more. Where the megalodon was found, therefore, depended more on the stage of life it was in and the prey it preferred. Adult megalodons preferred deeper waters where larger prey, such as dolphins and small whales, were abundant: juveniles preferred shallower waters, where they could feed on smaller cetaceans.

Modern sharks are actually considered to be opportunistic predators (this means that they take advantage of animals in distress, rather than hunting them down themselves). Yet the megalodon, with its powerful jaws, large, sharp teeth, formidable size and its speed through the water, is considered by many to be one of the most formidable carnivores ever to have lived. Its dominance allowed it to prey upon a wide range of sea dwellers, such as dolphins, whales, turtles and marine mammals. Some scientists believe that the megalodon might even have had cannibalistic tendencies!

Megalodons became extinct about two and-a-half million years ago. Many theories have proposed to explain this:
• Changes in marine geography.
• Oceanic cooling.
• Competition from other marine animals.
• A reduced food supply.

Whatever the explanation, the megalodon's legacy lives on. In 2014, the Discovery channel aired programmes such as "The Monster Shark Lives", and "Megalodon: The New Evidence", which satisfy people's fascination with this legendary sea monster.

To sum up, the megalodon was an apex predator which, if it had not become extinct millions of years ago, would most probably still be the king of the ocean. Perhaps we should be thankful, because if the megalodon did indeed exist today, and encountered a human as its prey, it wouldn't even need to use its formidable teeth: its mouth was so big, it could easily swallow a person whole!

*65 – 0 million years ago.

NEWSPAPER ARTICLE

DEFINITION: The usual purpose of a newspaper article is to inform readers, but it may also seek to interpret current events or to entertain.

PURPOSE: To inform readers about events or issues which are of current interest.

AUDIENCE: An intended readership. This differs from tabloid to broadsheet newspapers (or a school newspaper!) and as such, the style of writing will depend on the newspaper's target audience.

For the sake of brevity we have called this text type newspaper article, but it must be remembered that the principles of this text type apply to the whole spectrum of the news medium: internet/online reporting, broadcast journalism etc.

This chapter has been developed in collaboration with industry professionals to reflect the conventions and standards of news outlets.

SUGGESTED STIMULI & RELATED ACTIVITIES

Stimuli and activities for journalistic writing can be divided into four broad categories:

1. Experience-driven stimuli and activities

As a precursor to actual writing, experience-driven stimuli are essentially real-world situations of which the pupils have first-hand experience. These may include:

Interviewing newsworthy people, for example eyewitnesses to an event; a retiring headteacher; sports people, etc.
Being part of the editorial team of a school newspaper.
A trip out (essentially leading to a recount of that trip, but if written for a newspaper, following the appropriate **structural format** and **stylistic conventions** of that newspaper).

2. Outcome-driven stimuli / activities

Producing a school newspaper.
Producing a digital newspaper.
A script-prepared piece to camera which incorporates most of the language features of a written article.

3. Analysis-driven stimuli / activities

Reading and discussing suitable tabloid newspaper articles.
Reading and discussing suitable broadsheet newspaper articles.
Reading and discussing children's newspapers e.g. 'First News'.
Watching and analysing TV news and sports reports, or listening to broadcasts on the radio.
Peer-reviewing initial drafts of articles (functioning as a sub-editor).

4. Transformational response

Turning factual historical information into a newspaper report e.g. a news story about the beheading of Anne Boleyn.

Turning a spoken piece to camera into a written newspaper report or vice versa.

STRUCTURAL MODEL

As there is already an accepted language within the newspaper industry for the structural elements of a newspaper report, we have deliberately decided **not** to include *pupil 'access' language* in this model.

1. Headline

2. Byline

3. Intro

4. Body

5. Sources

6. Illustration + caption

Most newsworthy info
Who? What? When? Where? Why? How?

Important details

Other general info
Background
info

The industry standard is the 'inverted pyramid' model of writing a news story. The most important information appears right at the start of the piece. You tell the story, making sure the 5W's - What? Who? Where? When? Why? and How? are all covered, and leave the background and minor detail until the end.

Most 'straight' news and sports stories follow this structural pattern. You can, however, see deviation from this set standard in different types of news story, eg opinion, features, colour pieces, sidebars, case studies and picture captions.

Sources (quotes from people commenting on the event) may be included within the body. They can also conclude the newspaper article, but writers should avoid using really dramatic quotes right at the end - they should be further up the news story.

Structural model part 1: Headline

The opening structural element of a news article is the headline, which must always include or summarise the main points of the news story. Headlines are written to grab the attention of the reader. Please note that in the classroom there is no point telling pupils that it should be 'attention grabbing' if ways by which it is actually made 'attention grabbing' are not discussed. 'Attention grabbing' is an **outcome**: we should be sharing **ways of achieving outcomes** with pupils!

Effective headlines often trigger an emotional response (negative or positive depending on the content of the article). These include:

- Headlines which engender or provoke fear in the reader.
- Headlines which appeal to a need or desire of the reader.
- Headlines which use or feature facts or statistics to appeal to the curiosity of the reader.
- Headlines which are written as questions (positive or negative) which make the reader curious enough to read further.
- Headlines which are funny.

Language features:

1. Main point summary

A single sentence, made up of no more than seven words, sums up the main events of the story. The seven-word constraint is a useful writing challenge, as it makes pupils think carefully about vocabulary choices.
Tabloids are more likely to use capital letters for the whole of the headlines, especially on the front page main story. Inflammatory and provocative language is sometimes used to draw the reader in:

SEVENTEEN CARS STOLEN IN ONE SHOCKING NIGHT

- Crime Story

WORLD RECORD COOKIE BAKED IN LOCAL TOWN

- Human interest story

ALIEN LANDS! EVIDENCE FOUND IN COASTAL VILLAGE

- Sensational story

One golden rule, however, is not to mix upper and lower cases in headlines, e.g. Seventeen Cars Stolen In One Shocking Night.

2. Alliteration

Alliteration is the repetition of **sound** at the start of a series of words. This is a common feature of headlines. It is important to clarify that alliteration is not repetition of the same initial letter (e.g. thought and toad) but rather, repetition of an initial phoneme e.g. 'The wicked wizard went wild with wonder and whimsy'. It is useful to stick to the seven-words-or-less constraint, making it clear that not **every** word in the headline need start with the same sound:

Burglar **B**ill caught in **b**ank robbery **b**lunder

- Crime story

Cake **c**raze **c**atches on after **c**ooking **c**ompetition

- Local interest story

Poorly **p**erforming **p**oliticians **p**ut in their **p**lace

- National news story

3. Rhyme

Rhymes occur when the **final** sounds of a series of words are the same. This is another common headline technique, especially in sensationalist publications and tabloids. Stick to the seven-word maximum, and again, not every word has to rhyme:

Serious time for illegal climb

- Crime story

Scale-breaking whale injures his tail

- Environmental story

Prize mutt born to strut!

- Animal competition coverage

4. Puns

This technique employs words which sound alike but have different meanings. They are used to create funny or clever headlines, often linked to a well-known catchphrase. Like alliterative and rhyming headlines, these are found more often in tabloid newspapers.

UP TO ARREARS

- Financial story (The Sun)

EUSTON - WE HAVE A PROBLEM

- Local travel story (The London Paper)

RING IT ON!

- Olympics coverage (Daily Mail)

Headlines which use techniques like this will often have a subhead beneath, which clarifies the story the headline has referred to obliquely. Hence:

UP TO ARREARS
Camden leader steps down after deficit revealed

EUSTON - WE HAVE A PROBLEM
Travellers trapped in signal melt-down

RING IT ON!
Five more Olympic golds for Great Britain

5. Question

This method presents a summary of the article content in the form of a rhetorical question, simultaneously providing enough information to draw the reader in whilst also asking a question which prompts further reading. Within this technique there is an implied promise of an answer in the article (often there is actually no concrete answer, rather speculation and conjecture – this should be explored when reading examples). Again, the seven-word limit should be adhered to, with a question mark included at the end:

Did we really land on the moon?

- Government investigation

Is this the end for Jose Ferguson?

- Sports report

Can we trust doctors' orders?

- Health issue report

6. Emotive exclamation

This technique works by aligning reader and writer through the implication that the writer shares the same surprise, delight, moral outrage, anger or other heightened emotional state that they hope to evoke and inspire in the reader. Short, evocative phrases are commonly used, the content of which is often more vague than in other headlines. They are usually supported by a clear photograph and a sub-heading which clarifies the focus of the article. An exclamation mark may be included at the end:

IT'S A MIRACLE!

- Human interest story

WE ARE AT WAR!

- International news

DISGUSTING, EVIL AND SAVAGE!

- Political report

Structural model part 2: Byline

The byline is the name and position or job title of the person writing the article. (The easiest way to teach it is to explain that the byline is 'who it's **by**!').

Language features:

On a newspaper page layout, bylines are traditionally placed between the headline and the intro paragraph. They begin (unsurprisingly) with the word 'by', which can begin with either a capital 'B' or a lower case 'b'. In class, you may wish to decide which newspaper the pupils are writing for and research its 'house style' - the set of design and type rules each news outlet employs to ensure consistency. Usually, the pupil would include their own name, but if you'd like some fun, you could challenge them to come up with pun-based pseudonyms:

By Doug Updirt,   By Anita Story,   By Jean Pocket, Fashion Correspondent etc.

Structural model part 3: Intro

The intro paragraph (only one paragraph) is a synopsis of the whole news story. The easiest way to teach this is by using the five W's: Who, What, Where, When, Why. A brief detail related to each 'W' will suffice. Do not overdo your adjectives! The position of the W's within the paragraph relates to the content of the news story. In general, most news stories start with the What (happened). Celebrity stories will feature the Who first. Not may stories start with the Where because newspapers are more interested in people. For example: "Residents are up in arms at the news that a town centre nature reserve is to be turned into a car park".

The intro paragraph is often presented in a **bold** typeface. Sometimes the first letter of the first word of the intro paragraph will have a drop cap (a larger font with its base dropped below the line). Some newspapers favour the entire first word in capitals. It's all down to house style.

Language features:

1. The single sentence challenge

Most intros found in newspapers, especially tabloid publications, will only be one sentence long and yet will still manage to cover all of the five W's. Aim for a limit of 20 words per intro. One of the most useful ways to teach this skill is to look at real examples and ask pupils to identify each of the W's in the sentence. Intros focus very much on the What and include the other W's depending on relevance and significance For example, you could provide an intro like this:

JUBILANT Tories were celebrating in London this morning after pulling off a stunning general election victory.

Then, providing a 5W list, ask pupils to explain how each one has been covered:

Who: The Tories.
What: Were celebrating.
When: This morning.
Where: In London.
Why: Winning the general election.

This can also be a great comprehension exercise, as in many examples of the intro paragraph one or more of the W's is **inferred**. For example:

Two guard dogs, who protected Prince Dominic while he stayed at Camp Thaddion, have been given bravery awards.

…the *when* is not a specific measured time, but can still be identified as 'while he stayed'.

In this intro paragraph…

Racing superstar Max Speed celebrated his historic Grand Prix victory last night and has been tipped to receive a knighthood.

…the *where* is not made explicit, yet the inference could simply be 'at a party'.

2. How

In addition to the 5 W's, the intro paragraph may include a 'How' element if it is pertinent. This could still be worked into a single-sentence intro:

Champion cyclist Christie Jones was celebrating yesterday after using her new bike to set a world time-trial record at the Statonheim track in Holland.

Who: Christie Jones.
What: Broke world record.
When: Yesterday.
Where: On the Statonheim track in Holland.
Why: Setting a world time-trial
How: Using a new bike.

Pupils may also find examples of newspapers using a "standfirst" which is a separate introductory paragraph, usually but not always boxed off on the page. This allows the newspaper to "set the scene" if it is thought necessary. It's a stylistic device more often found on feature pages rather than news:

"Last week, 40 Afghan men were found dehydrated and starving in the back of a lorry in Dover. Our Current Affairs editor Sophie Diamond finds out why so many are willing to risk their lives getting in to the UK."

3. Start with a story

Once children have grasped the rules of creating very simple intros, they can be encouraged to extend their journalistic skills by taking a different approach to their first paragraphs.

This was the intro of the front page news story on 27th April 2015 in the Guardian. Two days earlier, the Nepalese earthquake had hit:

"The three sisters were doing what many children do at the weekend in south Asia: playing cricket. In the narrow alley outside their four-storey home, Kausis, Binu and Jyothi, aged eight, 10 and 12, sent an old rubber ball bouncing off the faded brick walls of the ageing houses of Bhaktapur, a World Heritage site known for its ancient architectural treasures that lies around 8 miles (13km) from Nepal's capital, Kathmandu."

To avoid a re-hash and repeat of the bare news facts, the reporter has started his intro with a "story". By focusing on the three children mentioned, the newspaper manages to keep the story fresh and takes a human interest standpoint. This technique needs to be modelled carefully, as genre confusion (narrative or news?) is a real possibility with less able pupils. But is it an incredibly useful and powerful way of rendering a news story. It is also a writing style that features writers often use.
We would suggest that children "start with a story" only when teachers are 100 per cent certain they know the difference between a news story and a narrative story!

Structural model part 4: Body

The body of the news story expands on each of the W's in the intro. All details must contribute to the 'So what?' - the so called 'Hidden W' of journalism. They should be pertinent, concise and information rich, so that the reader feels as informed as possible. This expanded content is usually written in short, clear and easily-digestible paragraphs of no more than 40 words each.

Language features:

1. Connectives

Often the structure of the body is either chronological; cause-and-effect or question-and-answer driven. As such, effective use of linking words and phrases is key. The analysis of an existing article and the subsequent creation of a **context-based** word display may be a useful preparatory activity:

Subsequently, all the offenders were captured and charged with robbery.

- Crime story

*Residents were puzzled by the delay **and,** after midnight, the missing fireworks were found in a park dustbin.*

- Local interest story

*Work continues today **as** firefighters struggle to control the forest blaze.*

- International story

2. Noun, who/which/where,

This sentence type is useful for conveying information succinctly in the body text as it includes a **subordinate clause.** This allows additional details to be integrated between commas, brackets or dashes, without breaking the flow of the writing:

*The painting, **which is more than 200 years old,** was transported to the gallery under armed guard.*

- National story

*Jack Flynn, **who recently joined the company,** was a key witness to the crime.*

- Crime report

*The town market, **where local companies trade at the weekend,** has become a hotspot for tourists.*

- Travel report

This technique is also useful as an editing tool. For example, if a pupil has written a sentence which starts with the subject (a very common occurrence!)…

The old man was eventually found in the park.

…you could challenge them to improve the sentence by turning it into a 'Noun, who/which/where,' essentially asking them to add extra information via the use of a subordinate clause. In this way they are employing grammar techniques to improve writing, which will in turn improve their knowledge of grammar terms and usage:

*The old man**, who had been missing for two days,** was eventually found in the park.*

3. Some; others

One key element that should prevail in journalistic writing is the inclusion of multiple, balanced perspectives. Of course, this does not always happen in the real world due to media bias and corporate or national agendas, but this should not discourage us from teaching pupils about objective, impartial writing. The 'Some; others' sentence allows for two opposing perspectives (separated by a semi-colon) to be presented concisely in one sentence:

Some residents believe that these new safety measures will reduce crime; others are not so hopeful.
- Crime report

Some park-goers queued for hours to get on the latest roller-coaster; others were content to ride the dodgems.
- Local interest story

Some companies have suggested that privatisation will lead to better services; other groups say treatment will become too expensive.
- Medical health report

4. Then and now

Another key feature of journalistic writing is the deliberate use of tense changes for effect. One common pattern is for the writer, or perhaps the news broadcaster, to comment first on how something **was**, and then follow up with how it is **now.** The 'Then and now' sentence type enables pupils to replicate this patterning in their writing through a variety of linking words and phrases:

Only weeks ago this was a peaceful village, now it stands in ruins, torn apart by military violence.

- War report

At first, witnesses believed the strange lights in the sky to be aeroplanes, but soon they realised the cause was much more sinister.

- Local phenomena report

In the 1980s, Detroit was a thriving city of industrial prosperity, now many factories lie dormant and abandoned.

- International finance report

5. V(ed) next V(ed)

Following the cause-and-effect patterning of journalistic writing, this fairly simple technique presents two actions in the same sentence, establishing a sequential link so that the reader knows **why** events happened as they did, in the order that they did. 'V' stands for 'verb', and the (ed) is included to remind pupils to use the past simple tense:

*Neighbours reported that Harold scream**ed** at the robbers and chas**ed** them down the road.*

- Local crime report

*Volunteer groups clear**ed** the park of rubbish, then pack**ed** up all the litter for recycling.*

- Local interest story

When teaching this technique it is important to point out that not all simple past-tense verbs end in 'ed', and the sentence name is simply a reminder, not a steadfast rule:

*The striker **ran** down the line and **sent** a perfect ball into the penalty area.*

- Sports report

Another important feature of many kinds of journalistic writing is the use of emotive words to provoke reader response. This sentence type can, therefore, be useful during the editing process, as pupils can be challenged to replace less effective verbs, expanding the verb phrase wherever possible. For example:

*Fans **cheered** when Plonaldo **walked** out for his final game.*

…could become…

*Fans **screamed with delight** when Plonaldo **strolled** out for his final game.*

6. Ending

There is no single correct way to end a news story. 'Straight' news stories generally end looking forward, eg

"Jenny is expected home from Nepal on Thursday."

"Little Jimmy is expected to get out of hospital next week".

Opinions and features can have more considered endings, as described below.

The use of a final memorable quote:

Mrs Redford added, "Things just won't be the same anymore, too much damage has been done. It is a terrible, terrible thing."

If Mrs Redford has been quoted earlier in the piece, this rounds the story off nicely.

A summary statement:

The worst of the weather has gone, but as repairs begin, residents in this small village will be feeling the effects for weeks to come.

These endings can be augmented with:

A play on the headline or intro (a complex form of ending which may expand wordplay used in the headline, or develop or linguistically play with a point from the first paragraph):

Headline: World record biscuit attempt ends in disaster

Closing line: *That's the way the cookie crumbles!*

A descriptive scene (which 'paints a word picture' for the reader).

Children are playing happily in the glorious sunshine as streets and parks are now clear of the rubbish that has plagued residents for so long. The community of Floundsworth village can be rightly proud of their collective efforts today.

Structural model part 5: Sources

Opinions and reports from experts, witnesses or other relevant parties are often included to lend authenticity and credence to a story. Although these are included here as a separate element, quotes should be integrated throughout the main body of the article.

Language features:

1. Direct speech

This technique involves using speech marks, or 'inverted commas', to mark the **actual words** spoken by a relevant party, verbatim. To facilitate the learning of the conventions of written speech, you could take the dialogue from a child-friendly news report and discuss how it would be written down accurately, using inverted commas and other appropriate punctuation. You could then expand this by talking about what details might be provided about the speaker (name, age, job, etc.) and the use of informal punctuation to mirror 'real' speech (e.g. the apostrophe for contraction). You could also point out that the use of the word 'said' is, in the case of journalistic writing, preferable to dramatic speaking verbs (due to the genre's factual nature):

Businessman David, 33, said, "I couldn't believe what I was seeing, the object flew down and swept up the ice cream truck before we even knew what was going on."

Kayleigh Jones, 23, who signed up to the programme this week, said, "It's a great way to keep fit and make new friends, I can't wait for the next session!"

"Something must be done, this is the third time this month," said James O'Neill, one of the forty residents affected by the flood.

2. Indirect speech

Also known as 'reported speech', this technique differs from direct as it does **not** include the actual words of the speaker written verbatim as a quote. Instead, the writer **paraphrases** what was said for the reader. One reason for using this technique is flexibility; it allows the writer to mould opinions and reports to suit their writing agenda, and to be vaguer with their sources where they see fit. One very effective way of teaching this is to take a quote that has already been recorded as direct speech, like the one below:

Businessman David, 33, said, "I couldn't believe what I was seeing, the object flew down and swept up the ice cream truck before we even knew what was going on."

…and demonstrate how it could be converted to indirect/reported speech by removing the inverted commas and changing some key words:

Businessman David, 33, told The Star that he couldn't believe what he was seeing, that the object flew down and swept up the ice cream truck before witnesses even knew what was going on.

In terms of grammar usage, this is a useful exercise, as it enables the teacher to draw attention to the changes in pronoun use ('I' to 'he', 'we' to 'witnesses') and the change in verb selection ('said' to 'told').

Direct
A military source said, "Unless the treaty is signed within the next 24 hours, we will be forced to take drastic action."

Indirect
Military sources say that unless the treaty is signed within the next 24 hours, they will be forced to take drastic action.

Direct

One customer said, "I have seen cockroaches in the toilets on more than one occasion."

Indirect

One customer reported seeing cockroaches in the toilets on more than one occasion.

Structural model part 6: Illustration + caption

These elements provide the reader with a visual aid which reinforces the content of the report. Large images are enhanced further with explanatory sentences that clarify and contextualise the visual. It is also worth noting that, alongside the headline, the image is often the first thing a reader will look at on a newspaper page, so it is important that a striking, meaningful and interesting image is selected, and explained effectively.

Language features:

1. Captions

Captions are presented directly under the photographs on the page. They are (generally) single sentences written in the present tense describing what is happening in the picture. The caption should not introduce any new information to the story.

De: de (Description: detail) sentences are ideal for captions. A short, sometimes capitalised description, is followed by a colon and a slightly more detailed sentence which adds to the story, sometimes containing a pun:

DEFLATED: Richard Branson's failed balloon attempt leaves him stranded.

INSIDE:
Celeb beauty secrets
Page 7

Tuesday 7th April, 2015

www.dailytrumpet.co.uk
@DailyTrumpet Price: 35p

DAILY TRUMPET

SCHOOL RUN IS 'FATAL'

Parents demand bus service

ANGRY parents have claimed their children's mile-long walk to an Avon primary school is "potentially fatal".

Mums and dads at Flinchester Primary, which has more than 450 children on roll, organised a protest march yesterday to launch a campaign to reinstate the school bus service.

About 400 parents waved banners, sounded air horns and brought traffic to a halt as they marched down Flinchester high street.

The march ended outside the council offices in the town square where the protestors handed in a petition demanding the reinstatement of the school bus service.

Stephanie Taylor, who has three children at the school, said: "Someone is going to be killed sooner or later. Something really needs to do something about this. It's a complete mess. We have ended up with the worst of both worlds – a dangerous pathway and no bus service at all."

Dangerous

Avon council scrapped the school bus in Flinchester last year but claim plans to create a new footway ran into financial trouble.

The council says its policy is to provide transport for pupils who live more two miles from school, unless the walking route is especially dangerous.

But an independent surveyor employed by concerned parents has now branded the existing pathway "potentially dangerous, possibly fatal".

Originally, council bosses planned to replace the pavements leading to the school in Sefton Avenue BEFORE the bus service was suspended.

But these plans ran into trouble when council budgets were frozen. Parents hope yesterday's protest march will lead to a rethink.

Teachers at the school are also concerned about the problem.

Headteacher Carole Summerson said that the situation was especially dangerous in the darker, winter mornings when children are making their way through the lanes leading to school.

JUST SAYING YES: Mums and dads call for the school bus to Flinchester Primary School to be reinstated.

"They are arriving late, cold, wet and miserable," she added. "It's not the best way to start a school day!"

An Avon council spokeswoman said the council was looking at school bus services to ensure that taxpayers' money is being spent wisely.

She said the council officers have been asked to assess the situation under new government learner travel guidelines.

And she added: "In addition, officers from the council's road safety team will be arranging with the school to raise awareness of road safety matters with the pupils as soon as possible."

Parents would also be able to request to accompany a risk assessor during an assessment of routes.

A "walking bus" for pupils has been organised by parents while discussions take place over restoring the bus service.

INSIDE THIS ISSUE
- **Letters to the editor Page 11**
- **Your problems Page 13**
- **What's on this weekend Page 22 and 23**
- **Sports special pull-out guide Page 32 and 33**

PERSUASIVE ESSAYS

DEFINITION: A persuasive essay is a piece of writing comprised of a structured argument for or against a specific point of view or issue.

PURPOSE: Reader yielding: to make the reader agree with the author's viewpoint.

AUDIENCE: The target audience is always those who reject, are ignorant of, or partially disagree with the author's viewpoint. This could be a small, specific group, concerned with a specialist issue, or it could be a wide-ranging audience involved in a national or global matter. With this in mind, technical language will be applied only in appropriate contexts.

SUGGESTED STIMULI & RELATED ACTIVITIES

There are five obvious categories of stimuli and activities for persuasive writing:

1. Hypothetical statement starters

These are best explained by way of modelled examples:

- Your teacher has decided to give you homework every night. Persuade your teacher that this is not a good idea.
- A litter problem is occurring at play times. Persuade other pupils to stop dropping litter.

2. Personal interest-linked stimuli

- Write an essay to convince your parents to let you have a pet. (...used with a pupil who likes animals.)
- Persuade other pupils why chess is an interesting hobby. (...used with a pupil who enjoys chess.)
- Think of an activity you enjoy. Persuade others to take up that activity. (...used with any pupil, as the generic nature of the activity allows pupils to personalise it.)
- Think of a club that you belong to. Persuade others to join that club.

(Note: Ensure that some of the stimuli **don't** include the word 'persuade' (such as the first example above). This allows the teacher to assess whether the pupil has understood that it is a persuasive writing task without overt use of the word 'Persuade'.)

3. A 'real world' issue of local significance (letter writing)

Examples include:

- Write a letter to the editor to the local paper to persuade people to oppose the proposed new supermarket.
- Write an open letter to persuade people to oppose the proposed banning of bicycles in the park.
- Write a letter to your local MP to oppose the proposed new motorway.
- Write a letter to your local MP to support plans for the new motorway.

A useful way to add an extra tier of challenge for more able pupils is to ask them to argue for the least popular option - see previous page.

4. An issue of national or global significance

Persuasive essays in this category relate to 'big picture' themes of wide-ranging importance. Themes to consider include:

- Famine.
- Climate change.
- Disarmament.
- Atomic Energy.
- Racism.
- Human Rights.

Many useful themes can be researched at the United Nations Global Issues website: www.un.org

5. A cross-curricular opportunity

There are many opportunities for persuasive writing across the curriculum. These include:

- In science - when studying nutrition and health: essays to persuade people to eat a healthy diet.
- In history - when studying the Victorian era: essays to persuade factory owners not to use child labour (these should include historically accurate information gleaned from reading about the period or subject).
- In geography - environmental issues provide a broad range of potential persuasive essay opportunities.
- In music or art - persuading others why they should listen to a particular piece of music OR look carefully at the work of a specific artist.

STRUCTURAL MODEL

Persuasive writing can be treated as either a linear or non-linear text type. We will therefore provide a linear structural model first, and then discuss a non-linear approach. Neither is preferable, though from experience we would suggest that staff consider taking a linear approach first, and gradually progress to a less tightly structured model.

Linear model:

Pupil 'access' language	Meta language
1. What I think	1. Statement of viewpoint
2. Why I think it 1	2. First supportive argument
3. Why I think it 2	3. Second supportive argument
4. Why I think it 3	4. Third supportive argument
5. What other people think	5. Acknowledgement of alternative perspective
6. Why I still think it	6. Reiteration of viewpoint

This is a slightly simplified version of Aristotle's original six-point structure: Exordium (overview); Narratio (current position); Diviso (a break down of areas to be discussed); Confirmatio (arguments supporting the position); Confutatio (counter position); Conclusio (Emotional / logical 'call to action').

Non-linear model:

The non-linear approach is best explained as a shape! Pupils should be taught to think of persuasive writing as diamond shaped: you start with the **point** (Statement of viewpoint or 'What I think' from the linear model) and end with the **point** (Reiteration of viewpoint or 'Why I still think it' from the linear model). The language features which make up the middle of the diamond may be written in any order. There is no preference, and the use of the language features is dictated by the flow of the writing.

START WITH THE POINT

OPENING

LANGUAGE FEATURES
IN ANY ORDER

MAIN BODY CONTENT

CLOSING

END WITH THE POINT

Structural model part 1: What I think (Opening)

The opening of a persuasive essay is a statement of the author's viewpoint. With younger pupils it is wise to be specific in relation to how this is achieved. A useful starting point could be as simple as:

• Start with 'I'.
• Don't use 'good' or 'bad'.

For example:

I think that banning bicycles in the park is a terrible idea, and I hope you will agree with my reasons.

Language features:

1. Double bind

The simple form above could be developed as pupils progress, so that the opening takes the form of a 'Double bind' - two questions which reference the opposite point of view, followed by the word 'No' and a statement of the author's viewpoint:

Are we a school who choose junk food from MacWonlands? Are we a school who choose junk food from Ken Tucker's Fried Chicken? No, in our school we choose healthy food, and in this essay I will persuade you why healthy food is a sensible choice for all schools.

2. Short story + bad ending + could/if sentence

A further progression would be to open with a short story explaining what might occur (by way of a narrative) if X does or does not occur. Again, an example is the best way to explain this:

John was a loving boy. He was loved by his mum, dad, gran, grandad and everyone who knew him. One day John set off for school, but when he came to a busy road, he stepped out without looking left or right. John was killed by a passing lorry.

Every day since then, he has been missed by everyone who knew him. This is exactly what could happen if the busy road is built in front of our school, and in this essay I will persuade you why this should never, ever occur.

3. Negative – positive questions

This technique uses rhetorical questions to engage the reader from the start. It presents them with two opposing perspectives in the form of deliberately biased questions. This gives the impression of 'free thought', as if the writer is asking them to consider these ideas evenly, but actually, through weighted language, it leaves the reader with little doubt as to which side they should agree with. The writer can then use this as their statement of viewpoint, before moving smoothly into their essay with a linking phrase:

Do you want ill health and an early death, or do you want to live a long, healthy life? The answer is obvious, and in this essay...

- Healthy lifestyle essay

Do we want tired, unmotivated pupils, or do we want happy, engaged learners?

- Subject-based essay

Do you want to wear the same old dreary uniform to school every day, or do you want to be able to wear whatever you feel like wearing?

- School-based essay

The order of the questions can also be inverted, presenting the positive first, followed by the negative:

Do you want to live in a peaceful, friendly village, or do you want to live in a noisy, congested location?

- Town planning essay

4. Tell: show 3;

This opener uses a versatile sentence structure (equally at home in non-fiction writing as in fiction work) to emphasise the importance of an issue or the potential consequences of an action. It starts with a statement of viewpoint and continues (after a colon) with three linked examples, after which the writer may use a linking phrase to lead into the main body of their essay:

Animal testing is barbaric: needless suffering is caused; irreparable damage is done; animals live and die in awful conditions. In this essay I will show how…

- *Animal welfare essay*

Wearing our own clothes to school is a great idea: pupils will be happy; parents will save money; children will be more comfortable.

- *School change essay*

Smoking is a terrible habit: it shortens your lifespan; it causes diseases; it even harms those nearby.

- *Anti-smoking essay*

5. When; when; when, then.

This technique combines the 'pattern of three' (used in the previous technique) with the mini-fiction style of method 2 to draw the reader in. Firstly, a picture of a negative situation is created using three examples beginning with 'when'. Next, a suggestion of change, beginning with 'then' is presented. Finally, a linking sentence leads into the main body of the essay:

When sea levels rise year on year; when animal habitats are lost; when extreme weather threatens our safety, then it is time to act on global warming. In this essay I will…

- *Eco action essay*

When crisp packets are found all over the playground; when food is being dropped on the canteen floor; when pencil shavings cover the classroom, then it is time to take responsibility for litter in our school. In this essay I will…

- School change essay

When children are targeted by others on the internet; when they become scared to use social media; when insults are posted online, then something more must be done about cyberbullying. In this essay I will…

- E-safety essay

(More opening strategies are discussed in the book 'Teaching Outstanding Persuasive Writing'. Alan Peat, Creative Educational Press Ltd., 2011)

Structural model parts 2, 3, 4: Why I think it 1, 2 and 3 (Main body content)

These are written in list form because, as discussed in the **non-linear** explanation, there is no preferential order. It is also important to point out that pupils do **not** need to use all of the language features listed here, but rather the ones which best suit the purpose of their essay. It is wise to treat this only as a **menu of possibilities**.

Language features:

1. How would you feel…?

This sentence starter can be modified, but essentially the technique involves an emotional appeal to the reader structured in the form of a rhetorical question. It involves the reader at a personal level as it addresses them directly and asks them to empathise. The technique is particularly effective when emotive topics, such as animal rights and health and safety, form the subject of the essay:

How would you feel if you were trapped in a cage and subjected to painful experiments?

- Animal testing essay

How would you feel if every time you walked to school you had to dodge dangerous, fast-moving traffic?

- Town planning essay

How would you feel if you were hunted for your skin and bones?

- Animal welfare essay

2. Getting worse

The technical term for this persuasive technique is 'dramatic heightening'. It could be taught as a useful extension of the 'How would you feel…?' method. Note again how well the *'rule of three'* works:

*How would you feel if you were **pierced**, **poisoned** or even **slaughtered** by scientists testing the latest beauty products?*

- Animal testing essay

*How would you feel if your child was **hurt, maimed** or even **killed** by a car on their way to school?*

- Town planning essay

*How would you feel if every day you had to run the risk of contracting **typhoid**, **dysentery** or **cholera** from drinking contaminated water?*

- World aid essay

Once this technique is understood it can be extended via the doubling up of the *'rule of three'* technique for additional dramatic emphasis:

*How would you feel if your child was **hurt, maimed** or even **killed** by a **speeding motorcycle, car**, or **articulated lorry** on their way to school?*

3. Certainty statements

'Certainty statements' leave no room for an alternative perspective in the reader's mind. They open with phrases such as *'There is no doubt…'*; *'No argument can be had…'*; *'It is 100 per cent certain that…'*, etc.:

There is no doubt that pupils would be much happier to come to school if they were allowed to bring their mobile phones.

- School change essay

No argument can be had with the idea that studying comics in school would raise pupil interest and motivation.

- Curriculum change essay

It is 100 per cent certain that if I was allowed a pet dog it would help me to be more responsible, as I would have to look after all of its needs.

- Personal appeal

4. 'ly' words

Adverbs of manner intensify the emotional impact of a verb:

*Users of the new motorway may drive dangerous**ly**.*

- Town planning essay

*Smoking is a dangerous habit: it can kill quick**ly**.*

- Anti-smoking essay

They can even be doubled for additional impact:

*Footballers are paid too much considering they often act irresponsib**ly** and childish**ly**.*

- Sports essay

*If pupils were allowed to take part in a rock climbing club they would behave safe**ly** and sensib**ly**.*

- School change essay

5. Experts

Reference to experts can lend credibility to a persuasive argument. The choice of expert will directly relate to the subject of the essay, and can include doctors, lawyers, professors etc. Further credibility can be achieved by directly quoting these experts and/or referring to length of service e.g.

I've been a leading expert in this field now for more than twenty years and in all of that time I can honestly say...

Ninety-five per cent of doctors agree that...

Professors have proven, through a ten-year, in-depth study, that...

6. Numbers

This language feature begins with simple numbers:

In local schools with roads near them there have been three people hurt by cars in the last year. In schools with no road near them, no-one was hurt.

This can then be developed to include statistics and perhaps be combined with a quote from an expert witness:

"In local schools with a major road within a 500m radius there has been a 16.9 per cent increase in asthma among 5-9 year-olds. In schools with no major road within a 1km radius this statistic drops to only 3 per cent" said Sir Harry Head, a leading Professor.

7. Same word before and after semicolon

Quite simply, the (emotive) word before the semicolon is the same (emotive) word after the semicolon. This adds 'persuasive punch' to the emotive language:

*Building a road near our school would be **disastrous; disastrous** for many, many reasons.*

- Town planning essay

*Studying films in school would be **fantastic; fantastic** as it would increase pupil enjoyment and engagement.*

- Curriculum change essay

*The practice of fracking is **terrible; terrible** due to the grave potential harm it can cause.*

- Eco-concern appeal

8. Same word end of two sentences.

A similar technique to *'Method 7'*, which adds variety in the shaping of the persuasive language and creates emphasis through repetition:

*Smoking can **kill**. Smoking will **kill**.*

- Anti-smoking essay

*Cosmetic testing is **barbaric**. All animal testing is **barbaric**.*

- Animal welfare appeal

*Drinking can be **dangerous**. All drugs can be **dangerous**.*

- Health essay

9. See, hear, smell, feel sentences

Multisensory appeal is a key element of effective persuasive writing. Using appropriate vocabulary, all senses can be appealed to in a way that provokes an empathetic response:

Sound: *There will be a chorus of disapproval if...*

Sight: *Their judgement is clouded...*

Touch: *To truly grasp the importance of...*

Smell: *If we want to catch the scent of victory then we must...*

Taste: *If we carry on with this plan it will leave a bad taste in the mouths of local residents...*

Structural model part 5: What other people think (Main body content)

Acknowledgement of the alternative perspective is an important aspect of a persuasive essay, though it should be noted this part of the text should **not** be given equal weight, or a different text type (a balanced argument) will be produced.

Language features:

1. Them and Us

This is a polarising technique, and to make it effective, consider applying the 1:3 rule: state **one** alternative argument, then counter it with **three** opposing arguments:

They say that if the road is constructed then we will arrive at school more quickly. We say that it would be hard to hear the teacher in class. We also say that part of the woodland outside of our school would need to be cut down, which would harm wildlife. Worse still is the fact that we could be knocked down crossing that road.

2. 'What they ignore/what they are ignorant of'

This technique opens with a partial acknowledgment of the alternative perspective but then goes on to identify a flaw within:

Some argue that smoking is a habit that only affects the user, and that people should be free to choose. What they are ignorant of is the terrible effect of second-hand smoke.

3. Concede ground – take the high ground

This makes the author appear reasonable, considered and objective, which leaves them in a wonderful position to take the high ground and stomp down on their opponent from above.

It may be argued that a road would lessen congestion and allow commuters to arrive at work as much as five minutes earlier a day. This is certainly a valuable and important point, but I would argue that saving human life is far more important!

Structural model part 6: Why I still think it (Closing)

There is no single correct way to conclude a persuasive essay, but there are two key components which are found in many conclusions:

A restating of the viewpoint of the author. Essentially this is a reiteration of the opening using different words. It is often written as a bullet pointed list, preceded by a summative phrase:

In conclusion, I believe that animal testing should be banned for the following reasons:

- *It causes needless painful suffering to animals.*
- *The benefits to human beings are not proven.*
- *Any benefits to human beings that animal testing might provide could be achieved via other methods.*

- Animal testing appeal

A 'call to action'. This can be thought of as a 'What we need to do now to make a difference' statement, and includes a direct instruction for the reader to follow:

Write to your MP now and demand that they oppose the plans for the new motorway.

- Local planning essay

Visit www.spana.org and sign the petition against animal testing.

- Animal testing appeal

Apply for your appeal pack now and start raising money for Water Aid.

- Charity appeal

An optional third element which can be added is a **'time is running out'** statement. This affirms the urgency of the situation via the use of time vocabulary:

Act now, before it is too late for change.

The clock is ticking... take action now.

(Note: the ellipsis mark is used to indicate a dramatic pause.)

Time is running out: if you do not make this change now, the opportunity will disappear forever.

Further closing strategies are detailed in the book 'Teaching Outstanding Persuasive Writing' by Alan Peat, Creative Educational Press Ltd., 2011

FLINCHESTER PRIMARY SCHOOL

SAY NO TO THE ROAD

John was a kind, caring boy who was full of life. He was loved by his mum, dad, baby sister and everyone who knew him. One morning, John said goodbye to his mum and set off as usual but, when he came to the busy road outside his school, he stepped out without looking left or right. John was killed by a passing lorry and, ever since that terrible day, he has been missed by everyone who knew him. This is exactly what could happen if the new road is built in front of Flinchester Primary School and in this essay I will persuade you why this should never, ever occur.

There is no doubt that the construction of a busy main road outside our school is a dangerous and potentially deadly idea. Currently, the roads around the school have sensible speed controls, effective parking restrictions and are used respectfully by local drivers, cyclists and pedestrians. A new main road, and the speeding traffic that comes with it, would increase the chance of accidents involving children immensely. According to the AA, about 5,000 children under the age of 16 die or are seriously injured on Britain's roads each year – how would you feel if your child became one of these statistics because they were hurt, maimed, or even killed on this new road?

It is also 100 per cent certain that the construction of a new road would create a constant distraction for children who are trying to learn and teachers who are trying to teach. Pupils would have to endure the daily racket of drills, lorries and diggers while the road was being built, only for that cacophony to be replaced by a never-ending stream of noisy, pollution-spewing traffic. Even the pollution itself would cause problems, as leading professor Sir Harry Head noted in his latest report: "In local schools with a major road within a 500m radius, there has been a 16.9% increase in asthma among 5-9 year-olds. In schools with no major road within a 1km radius, this statistic drops to only 3%." The facts speak for themselves.

Furthermore, any rational person must agree that planners and builders have acted rashly and thoughtlessly in their organisation of this road. The proposed road runs right through a wonderful grassy area; an area which is a popular place for the children of Flinchester Primary, as well as other local children, to meet, play and explore. Not to mention it being the habitat of local wildlife. Would you like it if someone bulldozed and paved over your home, just so people could get where they were going a little faster? If this plan goes ahead, it will certainly leave a terrible taste in the mouths of both young and older Flinchester residents alike.

It may be argued that a new road would ease village congestion and allow commuters to arrive at work as much as five minutes a day earlier. While this is certainly a valuable and important point, I would argue that the lives of young children, their ability to learn without interruption and the conservation of our local green areas, are all far more important!

In conclusion, I believe that plans for a new road outside Flinchester Primary School should be scrapped for the following reasons:

- The road would put the lives of young children at constant, needless risk.
- Pupils' learning and health would be adversely affected by the building and use of the road.
- A valuable, cherished, and well-used green area would be needlessly destroyed in the road's construction.

After having read all this information, I hope you agree that the new road is a dreadful idea. If so, please sign our online petition at *www.saynototheroad.com/Flinchester*.

The clock is ticking, act now… before it's too late!

BALANCED ARGUMENTS

DEFINITION: A balanced argument presents two or more contrasting perspectives with equal weight and no bias.

PURPOSE: To provide even coverage of the issue for discussion, which allows the reader to reach a balanced, informed judgement.

AUDIENCE: General, and as such, contextual information may have to be provided early on, and clear, jargon-free text will be used throughout so as to avoid alienating readers.

SUGGESTED STIMULI & RELATED ACTIVITIES

As an introduction to the writing of balanced arguments, pupils might consider a range of topics which engender widely different views, such as the treatment of animals in different contexts. They could explore areas like circuses and zoos, and whether or not animals should be kept as pets. This could be expanded with a look at online documentaries such as 'Blackfish' (based on the treatment of orca whales in captivity).

Once the idea of a contested topic is clear, pupils could consider news reports or debates in which representatives from opposing groups share their opinions, and respond to one another. They might also compare persuasive literature from local MPs.

Following this, pupils can research, prepare and debate a chosen issue as a class. This can begin with light-hearted, easily-relatable, school-based issues, such as:

- Should we do homework?
- Should all children walk to school?
- Should we be made to wear uniforms?
- Should we allow mobiles in class?
- Should we ban junk food in school?
- Should school days be longer?

And 'just for fun' issues like:

- Who is stronger, the Hulk or Superman?
- Would you rather be a vampire or a werewolf?
- Which is better, football or gaming?
- Would you rather be a bird or a fish?
- Do aliens exist?
- Burgers vs. pizzas
- Are ghosts real?

(Note: With most of the school-based issues, it is quite clear which stance the majority of pupils would initially take. However, the point of these early debates is to provoke a realisation. Pupils must recognise that in order to create a truly balanced argument, we must at times adopt a perspective that is not our own, empathising with those who hold different points of view to ours.)

Once the process of a debate is understood, then pupils can consider in detail wider and more complex issues, such as:

- Should the legal driving age be lowered?
- Should plans for a new building go ahead?
- Should cosmetics be tested on animals?
- Should violent sports be banned?
- Should schools allow social media access?
- Should all schools be single-gender?

Children's fiction which deals with difficult issues (bullying, ecological disasters, animal cruelty etc.) could also be used to stimulate debate.

During preparation for oral debate there will be opportunities to involve pupils in note-making; recording points of view on grids or in diagrams; interviewing; and associated researching skills.

Finally, using their understanding of the process necessary for creating a balanced verbal discussion, pupils can use the structures and language tips that follow in this chapter to write balanced arguments on a range of subjects. Further productive examples include:

- Should schools serve only vegetarian meals?
- Should university courses be free?
- Should bullying have legal consequences?
- Should national service be compulsory?
- Should pupils have after-school jobs?
- Should YouTube be accessible in school?
- Should all internet access be free?
- Are computers better than books?
- Should the voting age be lowered?
- Should cars be banned from city centres?
- Should joined writing be mandatory?
- Should classrooms have video cameras?

STRUCTURAL MODEL

Pupil 'access' language	Meta language
1. Title	1. Title – condensed version of the IFD
2. IFD (Issue For Discussion)	2. Expanded explanation of the issue for discussion
3. Arguments (Main body)	3. Presentation of the arguments for and against the IFD as well as alternative views if necessary
4. What I think / What do you think?	5. Final paragraph including a conclusion or a call to the reader to decide

The main body of a balanced argument usually contains at least six different points, three 'for', and three 'against' (although this can be altered if a range of perspectives are explored). The 'rule of three' is common in persuasive writing, and works just as well in a balanced argument. 'For', 'against' and 'mixed opinion' viewpoints can be presented in a variety of configurations:

Two halves:

1. For 1 (F1)
2. For 2 (F2)
3. For 3 (F3)
4. Against 1 (A1)
5. Against 2 (A2)
6. Against 3 (A3)

Alternating:

1. For 1 (F1)
2. Against 1 (A1)
3. For 2 (F2)
4. Against 2 (A2)
5. For 3 (F3)
6. Against 3 (A3)

Spectrum (for multiple perspectives):

1. For 1 (F1)
2. Against 1 (A1)
3. Unsure 1 (U1)
4. For 2 (F2)
5. Against 2 (A2)
6. Unsure 2 (U2)

While these structural models are helpful, the decision of which configuration to use will ultimately depend on the viewpoints the pupil has been given or identified. With this in mind, when planning the argument we must first examine the balance and variety of viewpoints.

In the simplest form of a balanced argument, each side will comprise of a **single group *or* individual** with a **range of reasons** which support their **one agreed, distinct perspective**, e.g.

IFD – The building of a motorway near the local school

For: | **Local Council**
Reasons (x3): | *It will decrease traffic on smaller roads*
 | *It will increase revenue for local shops*
 | *It will reduce journey time for commuters*

Against: | **Parents of pupils**
Reasons (x3): | *It will put children's safety at risk*
 | *It will distract classes from their work*
 | *It will increase traffic around the school*

A variation on this polar arrangement is groups comprised of **different people** with **different motivations**, but who still fall clearly into a 'for' or 'against' category, e.g.

IFD – The building of a motorway near the local school

For 1: | **Local Council**
Reason: | *It will decrease traffic on smaller roads.*

For 2: | **Shop owner**
Reason: | *It will increase revenue for their shop.*

For 3: | **Commuter**
Reason: | *It will reduce their journey time.*

Against 1: | **Parent**
Reason: | *It will put children's safety at risk.*

Against 2: | **Farmer**
Reason: | *It will cut through his land.*

Against 3: | **Teacher**
Reason: | *The noise will disturb their class.*

After having explored the various viewpoints, pupils could collate the information using a spider diagram. This process often clarifies which writing model better suits the range of viewpoints:

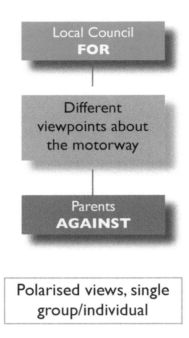

Polarised views, single group/individual

OR

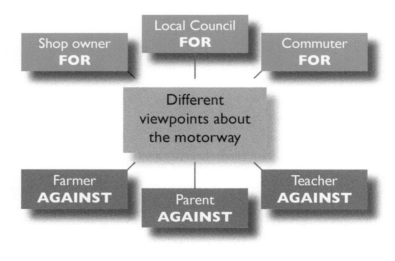

Polarised views, various groups/individuals

A visual mathematical model could also be used for separating and classifying perspectives. This is useful in terms of organising arguments and selecting structural models:

Polarised views, single group/individual

Polarised views, various groups/individuals

Not all arguments will be as clear cut as the previous example. Some issues engender both ardent support and vehement opposition (**groups** or **individuals**, with a **range of reasons** which support either their **single, clear** perspective or their **different, yet agreeing** perspectives). However, there may also those who hold a more neutral, or **uncertain** position:

IFD – The building of a motorway near the local school

For 1:   **Local Council**
Reason: *It will decrease traffic on smaller roads.*

For 2:   **Shop owner**
Reason: *It will increase revenue for their shop.*

Against 1:   **Parent of pupil**
Reason: *It will put children's safety at risk.*

Against 2:   **Farmer**
Reason: *It will cut through his land.*

Uncertain 1: **Local resident**
Reason: *Construction will be disruptive **but** traffic will be eased.*

Uncertain 2: **School Governor**
Reason: *Safety concerns will be raised **but** school access will be improved.*

(Note: the key use of the word **but** in the uncertain opinions, demonstrating the holder's conflicting beliefs)

When considering these more varied perspectives, the use of a spider diagram to collate and organise proves even more useful in terms of grouping ideas and selecting writing structures:

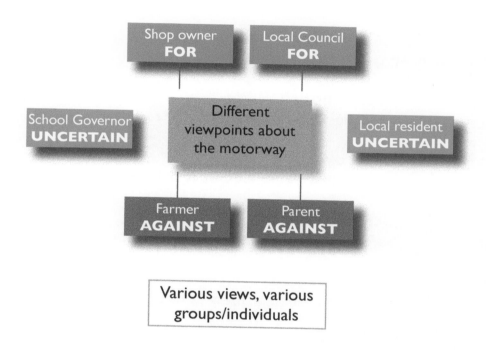

Various views, various groups/individuals

These varied perspectives can also be organised using a Venn-diagram style classification model, again useful for pupils when grouping arguments and planning writing:

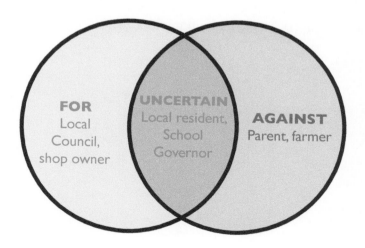

The more complex an issue is, the wider the range of viewpoints is likely to be. In a complex balanced argument, there will be a range of opinions that run the spectrum between 'for' and 'against'. Again, these may come from either **groups or individuals** with a **range of reasons** which support their **unique, individualised** perspectives e.g.

IFD – The building of a motorway near the local school

For 1:   **Local Council**
Reason: *It will decrease traffic on smaller roads.*

Partially for 1:   **Shop owner**
Reason: *It will increase revenue **but it might** take business elsewhere.*

Uncertain 1:   **School Governor**
Reason: *Safety concerns will be raised **but** school access will be improved.*

Against 1:   **Parent of pupil**
Reason: *It will put children's safety at risk.*

Partially against 1: Farmer
Reason: *It will cut through their land **but it might** improve delivery times.*

Uncertain 2:   **Local resident**
Reason: *Construction will be disruptive **but** traffic will be eased.*

(Note: the key use of the word **but** for those who are uncertain, demonstrating the holder's conflicting beliefs. Note also the use of the phrase **but it might** in the partial opinion, indicating a leaning towards 'for' or 'against' in their view.)

Once these opinions have been collated, and the subtle differences between them understood, pupils could again use a spider diagram to organise (and thereby aid) structural planning:

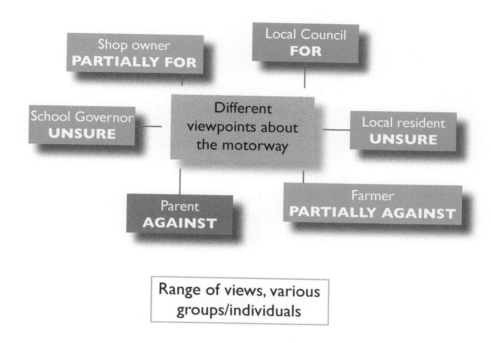

Range of views, various groups/individuals

This varied group of perspectives could also be visually organised using a continuum-based model:

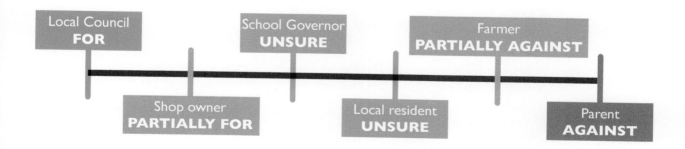

For such a varied selection of perspectives, the structural model for the 'Arguments' section of the text might be modified to look something like this:

Spectrum (for multiple perspectives):

1. For 1 (F1)
2. Partially for 1 (PF1)
3. Unsure 1 (U1)
4. Unsure 2 (U2)
5. Partially against 1 (PA1)
6. Against (A1)

(Note: If pupils internalise the 'access language' of the structural model and can talk through this in sequence, then they are free to concentrate on composition and effect - this is the same for **all** linear non-fiction text types.)

Structural model part 1: Title

The title should be a succinct summary of the 'issue for discussion' (IFD). It provides an opportunity to engage the reader immediately by framing the issue in an intriguing way.

Language features:

1. 3 Word Challenge.

To achieve this, pupils are challenged to take the issue for discussion and, having identified keywords, condense it to three words or less:

IFD: Should children have to work in silence at all times in the classroom?
Title: Silence in class.

IFD: Should pupils be allowed to study comics as part of their literacy lessons?
Title: Comic lessons.

IFD: Should the testing of cosmetic products on animals be banned?
Title: Animal testing.

2. (Verb)ing titles

Many balanced arguments are based on whether or not something should occur/be done. Opening with a direct naming of the contested action immediately makes the subject clear:

* *Variant 1: (Verb)ing a(n) object*
Building a motorway.
Creating a club.
Downloading a film.

* *Variant 2: (Verb)ing object*
Banning whaling.
Keeping orcas captive.
Charging bullies.

- *Variant 3: (Verb)ing the object*
Lowering the driving age.
Changing the speed limit.
Demolishing the park.

3. vs.

Short for 'versus', from the Latin for 'turned', vs. means 'against' or 'in contrast with'. It is a term that suits the purpose of a balanced argument perfectly, and can be used to good effect in a title which succinctly presents opposing ideas:

Free vs. Paid Education.

Capitalism vs. Communism.

Public Transport vs. Cars.

4. The question?

This title variant engages the reader by presenting the 'issue for discussion' in the form of a rhetorical question, encouraging them to formulate an initial opinion which may be modified by the subsequent debate:

Should school terms be longer?

Is it right to keep animals as pets?

Should national service be compulsory?

This title may be varied by presenting the topic's contrasting perspectives in the form of a question. Note the importance of the word 'or':

Mixed or single gender schools?

Fast food convenience or healthy eating effort?

Own clothes or uniform?

5. The issue:

This title, well-suited to journalistic content, opens with the simple declarative 'The issue', followed by a colon and statement of the issue. The topic element should be derived from the IFD and conveyed in three words or less:

The issue: phones in school.

The issue: longer school days.

The issue: is whaling justifiable?

The opening phrase can vary, as long as it is short and punchy:

The debate: free government Wi-Fi.

The problem: cyberbullying.

The argument: banning homework.

Structural Model part 2: The issue for discussion (IFD)

This structural section of the text is essentially an expansion of the title which gives the reader a clear, more detailed understanding of the focal topic. This might comprise of a general overview of the issue, or it may be a brief outline of the contesting ideas which will be elaborated upon in the main body of the text.

Language features:

1. The issue for discussion is, _____.

A simple starter based on the IFD abbreviation, this technique opens with the phrase 'The issue for discussion is,…', and continues with the matter being considered, without including the viewpoints of any contributors. It guides the reader into the text, allowing them to consider their own position first:

The issue for discussion is, should violent sports be banned?

The issue for discussion is, should pupils take after-school jobs?

The issue for discussion is, should England join the Euro?

Once this technique is established, the opening phrase could be varied:

The question being discussed is, should violent sports be banned?

The matter for debate is, should pupils take after school jobs?

The subject for debate is, should England join the Euro?

2. Some; others

This technique presents brief summaries of the opposing viewpoints which will be expanded upon in the main body of the text:

Some people believe that the legal driving age should be lowered; others think this would be an irresponsible move.

Some people think pupils should be financially rewarded for academic achievement; others think this would cause too many problems.

Some people think that boys and girls should attend separate schools; others think this would be socially damaging.

3. The issue of_____ is a 2A matter

This opener uses two neutral adjectives to describe the issue for discussion:

The issue of the new motorway is a complex, important matter.

The issue of school uniforms is a recurrent, significant matter.

The writer could, from the outset, use this as an opportunity to suggest their own personal stance:

The issue of fox hunting is a controversial, violent matter.

The issue of criminal punishment is a murky, unclear matter.

4. Today's issue for discussion:

This opening, best described by way of examples, is particularly useful for generating discussion about the use of a range of punctuation (apostrophe for possession, colon, and question mark):

Today's issue for discussion: should fast food television advertising be banned?

Today's issue for discussion: should cosmetic products be tested on animals?

Today's issue for discussion: should all forms of music downloading be made free?

5. Shakespeare: IFD

Based on the opening line of the famous soliloquy in Hamlet, this 'nod to William Shakespeare' phrases the IFD in the well-known rhetorical pattern to give gravitas to the debate:

To ban jewellery in school or not to ban jewellery: that is the question.

To reinstate the death penalty or not to reinstate the death penalty: that is the question.

To make cursive writing mandatory for all or not to make cursive mandatory: that is the question.

This technique is best used with issues that have a long history of prior debate, and goes some way towards conveying that the matter is perennially challenging to resolve. This may be used seriously for subjects of great import (as with the death penalty), or whimsically for trivial matters (jewellery in schools).

6. What if? Today we discuss

Opening with the phrase 'What if?', this technique presents the issue for discussion in the form of a hypothetical situation, then continues with an inclusive statement that sets out the intention of the piece:

What if the price of petrol doubled? Today we discuss the possible consequences of such a decision.

What if all school children were served vegetarian meals? Today we discuss the pros and cons of such a change.

What if university courses were free? Today we discuss the possibilities of this change.

7. Tabled

This final technique uses the operative term 'tabled' (meaning to present formally for discussion or consideration at a meeting) to present the issue for discussion in a business-like manner:

The following issue has been tabled: increased tax rates for high-level earners.

The following issue has been tabled: compulsory national service.

The following issue has been tabled: raising the price of junk food.

Structural model part 3: Arguments

This is the main body of the text, in which the various viewpoints are presented. In the simplest form of balanced argument, these are usually grouped 'for' and 'against'. But opinions can vary greatly, and the degree of variation will dictate the arrangement of the arguments. Generally, however, there are three main 'categories' of opinion:

STRONG   MODERATE   UNCERTAIN

We will use these colour-coded categories throughout this section to help link appropriate language techniques to each category.

Language features:

1. No doubt sentences (STRONG)

These sentences employ a range of 'certainty statements' to present ideas as undeniable and inarguable. They suggest strong, unwavering opinions:

Local farmers say there is no doubt that the new road will cause chaos.

Teachers say that the negative impact of mobile phones in the classroom is a proven fact.

Children at the school claim it is undeniable that comic lessons would increase their enjoyment.

2. Consequence sentences (STRONG/MODERATE/UNCERTAIN)

Useful for all three categories, this technique presents hypothetical consequences of the proposed change (negative, positive, or merely to provoke thought) as part of the argument:

STRONG
Supporters say that if whaling continues, a majestic species may soon be wiped out.

MODERATE
Local shopkeepers have suggested that if the new road is opened, customers could be taken away to bigger supermarkets.

UNCERTAIN
Even though they admit that technology is important in school, parents are concerned that too much time spent on computers could damage writing skills.

3. The more, the more sentences (STRONG/MODERATE/UNCERTAIN)

Linked to the previous technique, this method presents potential consequences using a clear 'cause and effect' structure:

STRONG
Teachers have warned parents that the more pupils bring tablets into school, the more their learning will be disrupted.

MODERATE
Politicians argue that the more high earners are taxed, the more chance there is of them finding ways to avoid paying what they should.

UNCERTAIN
Local ecologists have predicted that the more trees are removed from the area, the more likely it is that animal habitats will be lost.

Once this technique is grasped, the linking words can be changed for variety or appropriateness:

*Teachers have warned parents that the **more** pupils bring tablets into school, the **less** they will concentrate in class.*

4. 'Not only is' sentences (STRONG)

Useful when strong opinions are held, this technique opens with the phrase 'Not only is', and continues with two consecutive arguments:

Not only is recycling great for the environment, eco groups say it also helps to save money.

Not only is fox hunting a cruel sport, animal rights groups claim it is an ineffective means of population control.

Not only is junk food a clear cause of weight-gain, scientists say it can also affect your heart.

5. No answer questions (STRONG)

This method uses a rhetorical question (one that requires **no answer**) to make the reader think about the hypothetical (and often exaggerated) consequences of a proposed action. It works particularly well when tagged onto a strong opinion:

How could we knowingly force pupils to do more work?

Do we really want young adults called into military action?

Can you imagine the problems working parents would face if school terms were decreased?

How would you feel if you were hunted tirelessly by greedy poachers?

This technique could also be used for those who hold an **uncertain** position, to present hypothetical consequences in the form of rhetorical questions:

How do you know that the new park won't cause a rise in truancy levels?

What if pupils were to lose their mobile phones on school grounds?

Is it possible that the new bypass will take business away from local shops?

6. 'An alternative' sentences (UNCERTAIN)

Useful for those who hold a neutral position, this technique allows contributors to provide a palatable alternative to those who hold polarised views:

An alternative to banning phones in school is to limit their use on certain days.

An alternative to keeping pets is to open farms to the public and allow volunteer groups to care for animals.

An alternative to banning fast food adverts is to limit their transmission to after the watershed.

7. Might sentences (MODERATE/UNCERTAIN)

A useful technique for conveying varying perspectives, this sentence employs the key word 'might' to present dual possibilities:

Although the motorway would reduce town traffic, it might cause more high speed accidents.

On the one hand compulsory national service may provide useful life skills, but on the other it might not suit every individual.

Some people think single-gender schools would cause group problems, yet on the contrary it might improve social relationships.

8. BOYS sentences (STRONG/MODERATE/UNCERTAIN)

This useful mnemonic device serves to remind students to distinguish between connectives, for effect, in their writing:

B: *Holidays are important, but pupils should be learning all year round.*

O: *The school day could be extended, or school holidays could be shortened.*

Y: *Foxes can be a menace, yet that does not justify their violent slaughter.*

S: *Pupils do not enjoy homework, so they should not be forced to do it.*

9. Getting worse/getting better sentences (STRONG/MODERATE/ UNCERTAIN)

This technique employs comparative and superlative adjectives to emphasise a particular viewpoint:

Computer games in school are bad, tablets are even worse, but mobile phones are the worst distraction of all. (Getting worse)

Playing together is good, exercise is better, but avoiding junk food is the best decision we can help pupils to make. (Getting better)

Once the idea of this construction is grasped, the comparative terms can be changed to include hypothetical 'getting worse' or 'getting better' scenarios:

What if a pupil was hurt, maimed or killed by a car on the proposed new road? (Getting worse)

10. Imagine + question? sentences (STRONG/MODERATE)

This technique employs a rhetorical question, coupled with a hypothetical suggestion (beginning with the word 'imagine'). These work together to engage the reader's emotions or senses in the reasoning process:

Imagine a class full of pupils all distracted by endless notification alerts. How would they possibly concentrate on their work?

Imagine being hunted every day for your skin and bones. How would you feel?

Imagine a school full of neatly dressed, smart pupils. Doesn't that sound wonderful?

11. Facts and examples (STRONG/MODERATE/UNCERTAIN)

This method encourages writers to support viewpoints with either fictitious or (preferably) genuine facts and figures. It lends itself to research projects; sourcing, searching and interviewing for information as preparatory writing exercises. Writers should also employ appropriate units to convey information accurately:

STRONG
Japan has needlessly slaughtered 8,201 innocent minke whales in the Antarctic for "scientific purposes" since the suspension in 1986.

MODERATE
UK households produced 30.5 million tonnes of waste in 2003/04, of which only 17 per cent was collected for recycling.

UNCERTAIN
More than 1.2 million people die in road traffic crashes every year, yet statistically Britain has the safest motorways in Europe.

12. Attack the facts (STRONG/MODERATE/UNCERTAIN)

This techniques works in opposition to the previous method, as the 'facts' presented this time contradict those provided by the opposing side:

Local councillors claim that the demolition will provide space for 40 new houses, yet house provision in their previous development project came up short by 25 per cent.

Hunting supporters claim that it is an effective way to control the fox population, yet five times as many foxes die on British roads, and their numbers remain stable.

13. Compromise (UNCERTAIN)

This technique uses a rhetorical question to present a position which may be agreeable to both sides:

What if breaks were shortened, rather than extending the school day?

How about a trial period for own clothes in school?

Would it be possible to build the motorway on a less intrusive route?

14. List words (STRONG/MODERATE/UNCERTAIN)

A simple technique which is useful for presenting one viewpoint in a linear manner:

Firstly, if the school day was extended, pupils would become tired and frustrated.

Secondly, parents would have to change their working patterns in order to collect their children on time, which may also have cost implications.

Thirdly, teachers would have even less time to plan lessons and assess work properly.

15. In other words (STRONG/MODERATE/UNCERTAIN)

In this technique, a particular viewpoint is presented twice; first at length, then summatively – often in an emotive or leading way. These are joined by a key linking phrase such as 'in other words'. This serves to emphasise the point:

Junk food can contribute to weight gain and heart problems. In other words, it is the last thing we should be encouraging children to eat.

The new motorway will increase the risk of property damage, injuries and fatalities. To put it more simply, it is a tragedy waiting to happen.

Pupils will be motivated by financial reward, just as in their future professional lives. In short, this will give them a taste of real world progression.

16. Results (STRONG/MODERATE/UNCERTAIN)

This final technique works by making a prediction about the outcome of either a presented perspective (i.e. the speaker's own) or an argument, but presenting it as fact, using certainty statements such as 'will be':

If the legal driving age is lowered, the result will be a rise in accident rates and subsequent insurance costs.

If homework is banned, it follows that pupils will learn less, and will be less prepared for the challenges of high school.

The new park will boost enthusiasm for exercise, increase fitness, and lower health problems.

Structural model 4: What I think / What do you think?

This final section summarises the various perspectives and concludes with either a statement of the writer's personal position (What I think) or an invitation to the reader to form their own opinion based upon the information gleaned from the essay (What do you think?).

Language features:

1. What I think sentences

Opening with a statement indicating that all viewpoints have been considered, this sentence type concludes with a statement of the writer's own position/stance:

After weighing the evidence, I think that plans for the new motorway should be scrapped.

Although arguments are strong on both sides, I think that pupils should be allowed to wear their own clothes to school.

Personally, I think that enforced military service is not a sensible choice.

This sentence type can be expanded by adding a justification statement which begins with either 'because' or 'as':

After weighing the evidence, I think that plans for the new motorway should be scrapped, as the potential for accidents and injuries overshadows the transport benefits.

2. What do you think? sentences

Beginning in a similar manner to the previous technique (with a statement that conveys the idea that all points of view have been considered) this sentence then concludes by inviting the reader to make up their mind:

After hearing both sides of the argument, it's up to you to make up your mind about the issue of whaling.

Both sides raise valid points. You will now have to weigh them up and decide for yourself whether fox hunting should continue.

The issue of national service is complex and personal. What do you think?

3. Most important – in short sentences

This technique can be used in the context of either the 'What I think' or the 'What do you think?' ending. It works by reiterating the complexity of the issue (using the phrase 'in short' to conclude), then closes with either the writer's position (A) or a call to the reader to make up their own mind (B):

(A) The issue of animal testing is full of questions, conflicting ideas and passionate opinions – in short it is a complex matter. I think that animal testing is unnecessary, and manufacturers should invest more money in alternate methods of testing.

(B) The matter of whaling is full of legal ambiguity, cultural issues and divided opinions – in short it is a hotly contested issue. Considering the points presented here, what do you think?

4. If...then..so/but sentences

This method can be used for both the *What I think* and the *What do you think?* closing variations. It works by presenting a potential consequence with a subsequent decision or call to decide:

If the motorway is built, then children will get to school quicker, so I think the plans should go ahead.

If the motorway is built, then children will get to school quicker, but their safety may be in danger. So, what do you think?

5. BOYS sentences

In terms of summarising and comparing points from the main body of the text, this technique again proves useful:

B: *Teachers know holidays are important, **but** think pupils should be learning all year round.*

O: *Councillors have suggested the school day could be extended, **or** school holidays could be shortened.*

Y: *Local people know foxes can be a menace,* **yet** *they maintain that that does not justify their violent slaughter.*

S: *Pupils do not enjoy homework,* **so** *they say they should not be forced to do it.*

6. Some: others. I/You? sentences

This sentence type helps the reader to summarise the main viewpoints succinctly (using 'some', a colon, then 'others'). The subsequent sentence is either a statement of the writer's own opinion, or a call to the reader to form their own:

Some people think that school days should be lengthened: others think this is a terrible idea. I think that school days are long enough, provided that they are packed with fun, engaging learning.

Some people think that school days should be lengthened: others think this is a terrible idea. After reading the different arguments, what do you think?

7. Bullet point summary

Here the main arguments are summarised using bullet points. Subsequently, the writer will include their final decision, or will call on the reader to make up his/her own mind:

To conclude, those who support fox hunting believe:
- *Foxes are pests.*
- *Fox numbers need to be controlled.*
- *Foxes attack farm animals.*

While those who oppose fox hunting believe:
- *Foxes suffer needlessly during hunts.*
- *The fox population is already under control.*
- *Farms can be easily secured against foxes.*

Personally, I think that fox hunting should be banned as it is a form of animal cruelty.

-or-

What do you think?

8. Alternative sentences

This method opens with a summary of the presented opinions. It then concludes with an alternative perspective which has not yet been considered:

Teachers think that cursive writing would look neat in books, yet some children may be upset if they struggle to change. However, I think the focus should be on typing skills, as they are much more likely to need these in their future jobs.

Even though people are allowed to drive at 17, some believe the age should be lowered to allow young people to drive as soon as they leave high school. However, I think the legal age should be raised, so as to avoid young drivers being forced into insurance fraud by high prices.

Parents claim the new park would provide children with a safe place to play, though the loss of the bowling green may upset older people. Perhaps instead, planners should invest more time into finding an alternate location for the new park.

9. Social media and web links

This final technique lends pupils' writing a contemporary feel as it provides opportunities for 'real' interaction and response, rather than a discourse which concludes with a (sometimes tokenistic) 'what do you think?'. Resources are provided which enable readers to discover more information about the topic, and suggestions of ways in which the reader can share and develop their opinion are also given:

To find out more and to contribute to the orca captivity debate, visit http://blackfishmovie.com

Add your thoughts and opinions to the discussion at www.bookface.com/foxornot

You've heard the arguments, now share your opinion! Tweep @thefoxproblem using the hashtag #foxwatch

(Note: This also provides an opportunity for e-safety discussion.)

The issue: Animals in Zoos

The issue of animal captivity is a difficult, complex matter. Some believe that captivity of any kind is a breach of fundamental animal rights; others see zoos as a sanctuary for endangered species and a means of educating the public with regard to animal welfare. Read on to find out about both sides of the argument.

Supporters of zoos believe that they are a valued tradition: a wholesome, educational family day out which is more personal and more memorable than reading a nature book or watching a documentary. They suggest that the closer together people and animals are brought, the better people's appreciation and knowledge of animals will be. Of 1000 large animal collections across the world, 80 per cent are in major cities. As such, not only do people gain a better appreciation of the animals they have the chance to see, zoo supporters suggest that the experience will motivate them to protect animals in the future.

Imagine if you were one of the last of your species, mercilessly hunted by poachers, struggling to find a safe habitat. Zoo supporters would point out that zoos aid endangered species by providing a safe environment where they are protected from such threats, as well as from starvation and predators. They also say that rehabilitation and breeding programmes for endangered species which might have trouble surviving, finding mates and breeding in the wild are important functions of zoos. In other words, zoos help endangered species avoid extinction: how can that be a negative thing?

Finally, zoo supporters would point out the fact that zoos are heavily regulated: reputable zoos are accredited by organisations like the Association of Zoos and Aquariums, which ensure that animals are being treated correctly. Even if the zoo is unaccredited, it will be regulated by animal welfare organisations, which establish standards for care. If the zoo meets these standards, then it is guaranteed to provide rich, spacious, engaging habitats in which animals are well cared for.

Those who are against the practice of keeping animals in zoos would argue that people have the alternative of seeing wild animals in real life by observing them in their natural habitats, or by visiting a sanctuary. Sanctuaries rehabilitate animals and care for surplus wildlife, unwanted exotic pets, or injured animals who can no longer survive in the wild, yet they do not buy, sell, or breed animals like zoos do. Zoo detractors would point out the fact that the vast majority of captive breeding programmes fail to return animals into the wild. Offspring usually become part of the zoo, or worse, a circus, petting zoo, or the pet trade, where they are bought, sold and bartered for, with little to no protective regulation.

Zoo detractors would also argue that while the draw of baby animals might increase the number of visitors to zoos, the enticement to breed lots of new baby animals soon leads to overpopulation. There is no doubt that some zoos destroy these 'surplus' animals outright: even 'regulated' and 'accredited' zoos are guilty of this practice. Those who are against zoos would highlight a CAPS (Captive Animals Protection Society) study, which found that at least 7,500 animals (perhaps even as many as 200,000) in European zoos are 'surplus' at any one time. In early 2014, there was a global outcry when a healthy young giraffe called Marius was killed in a Copenhagen Zoo, simply because he was 'surplus'. It was later admitted by zoo spokespeople that thousands of healthy animals are deliberately killed in European zoos each year.

Finally, imagine if you were trapped in the same room your whole life – would you be happy? Zoo detractors claim that due to their confined habitats, animals in captivity suffer from boredom and stress. No pen, no matter how spacious and well-equipped, and not even a drive-through safari, can match the freedom of the wild. Zoo detractors say that not only is a zoo an unhealthy place for animals, it is also a place where visitors, including children, are given the message that imprisoning animals for entertainment is OK.

To conclude, those who support zoos believe:
*   They increase the public's awareness of animal care and conservation.
*   They help keep endangered species from extinction.
*   They are heavily regulated and kept to high standards.

While those who are against keeping animals in zoos believe:
*   Sanctuaries are a much better, more effective alterative.
*   Zoos breed 'surplus' animals, which are dealt with terribly.
*   Zoos are confined, unstimulating environments in which to keep wild animals.

What do you think?

To find out more and contribute to the captivity debate, visit *www.captiveanimals.org*
You can also tweet your opinion @captiveanimals using the hashtag #ZooOrNoZoo

PERSUASIVE ADVERTS

DEFINITION: An announcement, often including mixed media, published via broadcast, print or electronic channels to a persuasive end.

PURPOSE: To arrest attention, engage the reader, and motivate them to do something.

AUDIENCE: Written for a wide spectrum of audiences, and for a wealth of purposes and products. Of all the text types covered in this book, this is the form most prevalent in today's society, and the one we are most likely to encounter on a daily basis. Technical language should only be used when it is context-specific and appropriate for the intended audience.

SUGGESTED STIMULI & RELATED ACTIVITIES

The study of persuasive adverts transcends the confines of literacy; it is crucial to the development of pupils' financial, social, and behavioural awareness. These adverts permeate our daily lives: we encounter them from the moment we switch on a television or radio, or pick up a magazine, newspaper, or even our mail. When we step outside they are all around us: on billboards, buses, shop windows, etc. All this before we have even ventured anywhere near our mobile devices and computers to access our most prevalent and popular source of information – the internet. As soon as we do, we are bombarded with adverts trying to convince us to do something, buy something, vote for something or ask for something. Pupils need to consider persuasive advertising in both a critical and reflective manner, rather than assuming the position of passive recipients of this media barrage.

Here are some preliminary activities which will help to achieve this aim:

- Before looking at any language features or advert examples, ask pupils to map their journey to school, identifying where and how often they encounter persuasive adverts.

- Once they have an approximate idea, ask them the next morning to try to keep an actual record, primarily of **how many** adverts, and if possible, **where** they were located and what product or position they were supporting or opposing. This activity may illustrate the prevalence of persuasive adverts, and will form an effective rationale for the study of the genre – facilitating a discussion of **why** studying adverts is so important. That is, to become discerning users of visual literacy and to be aware of companies trying to influence us throughout our lives, especially to do something that may be against our best interests, i.e. gambling, drinking alcohol, taking out high-cost loans etc.

- Ask pupils to collect examples of persuasive adverts to study in class. Challenge pupils to find examples of adverts for different products (from a range of sources) with varied target audiences. When analysed in class, a discussion of how different audiences are targeted and addressed will develop critical awareness of the genre.

- As a class, discuss which websites the pupils often use and visit them together. However, instead of looking at the main content of the site, analyse the advertising hosted there. What is being advertised? Why have the advertisers chosen that website? How much of the page is dedicated to adverts? These questions can lead to a discussion of website advertising revenue, how advertisers target their audiences, and even how websites track browsing history through 'cookies', tailoring adverts to single users so as to be ever more effective in influencing their behaviour.

Having considered these issues, pupils will be much more likely to transfer the outcomes into the persuasive adverts they create; analysing source material objectively and harnessing knowledge of how advertisers target their audiences. They will also have a greater awareness of how they, as consumers, are influenced by advertising, and will hopefully be less susceptible to negative persuasive media pressures.

STRUCTURAL MODEL

Every persuasive advert is a unique combination of many different components. Some may be simple, and contain relatively few elements:

Others may contain a much wider range of persuasive elements:

The composition of a persuasive advert, therefore, depends not on a strict structural model, but on a set of key factors:

- Audience – **who** is the advert aimed at?
- Intention – what is the advert's **intended outcome**?
- Existing knowledge – how much **new information** does the reader need?
- Placement – **where** will the audience see this advert? This is an important consideration: someone driving at speed past a billboard on a motorway will have much less time to absorb information than someone casually reading a magazine in their living room.

Throughout this chapter we will use these key factors to identify techniques which work well in a variety of settings, with a range of products, and with different target audiences.

With that said, regardless of context and target audience, the vast majority of persuasive adverts do have three key aims:

1. **Engagement** (grabbing attention and appealing to the reader)
2. **Persuasion** (convincing the reader)
3. **Information** (providing the reader with what they need to know)

As such, we will use these three key aims in place of a procedural structural model, under which we will group the following writing techniques:

Structural Model Part 1: Engagement
1. **Headers**
2. **Straplines / mottos / slogans**
3. **Wordplay and puns**
4. **Images**

Structural model part 2: Persuasion
5. **Product claims**
6. **Offers**
7. **Calls to action**

Structural model part 3: Information
8. **Dates, times and product information**
9. **Fine print**
10. **Web links and social media**

These techniques can be selected and combined in different ways to suit the audience, intention, prior awareness and placement of the advertised product in order to create the most effective texts.

Structural Model Part 1: Engagement

These initial elements serve to captivate and engage the reader. They are usually the first thing a reader will notice, and therefore serve to create an instant link between the product or service being advertised and the reader's needs.

1. Headers

Text-based elements that deliver a succinct, impactful message. Usually presented in a large, interesting font, in an eye-catching position.

Summary of product

Using a maximum of three words, this header-type encapsulates the unique selling point of the product. This encourages pupils to use high-impact language which is 'to-the-point':

UNLIMITED FILMS

- *Cinema promotion*

YOUR FILES, ANYWHERE

- *Software advertisement*

HEALTHY HAPPY HEART

- *Dietary advice poster*

Quote

This technique works by quoting the opinion of a user or beneficiary of the product being advertised, thereby demonstrating its effectiveness in a personalised manner:

"I'm so glad to have a warm bed to sleep in."

- *Animal welfare advert*

"I lost 3 stone – you can too!"

- *Weight loss campaign*

"A chilling, five-star thrill-ride."

- *Movie promotion*

Question?

This technique employs a rhetorical question which addresses the reader directly and either appeals to, or challenges, their existing ideas:

Tired of getting ripped off by mechanics?

- Car garage advert

Want a quick way out of debt?

- Financial services offer

Got something to sell?

- Online marketplace promotion

Time...name

Useful for discussing the purpose of the ellipsis mark, this technique sets out a general time frame and builds anticipation through use of exciting vocabulary and a dramatic pause (as indicated by the ellipsis mark):

Coming soon... the Flyson 350.

- Vacuum advert

It's here... unlimited gaming on your mobile!

- Mobile gaming promotion

Prepare yourself... the internet revolution begins!

- Broadband announcement

Calls to action

The opening of a persuasive advert with a 'call to action' creates a sense of both urgent anticipation and excitement:

Escape into a world of fantasy!

- Streaming movie service

Study for a brighter future at Fullster University.

- Higher education promotion

Sell your unwanted furniture!

- Online marketplace promotion

2. Straplines / mottos / slogans

Straplines, mottos and slogans are longer text-based elements of the persuasive advert which expand on the unique selling point of the product or service. They often contain a recognisable brand message. Pupils will know many of these off by heart – a class competition would generate a useful bank to analyse. There are also several handy slogan-creators online – simply search for 'slogan creator' to find them.

Claim of quality

This technique talks in complimentary and superlative terms about the product or service being advertised, setting it apart from the competition in general terms:

The best a man can get.

- Gillette

They're greeeeeeat!

- Kellogg's Frosties

It's finger lickin' good.

- KFC

Motivational catchphrases

Motivational catchphrases employ emotive, aspirational vocabulary. Their job is to make readers associate the values in the phrase with the company or product. They often appeal to a reader's competitive nature, hence their prevalence in sporting brand adverts:

Impossible is nothing.

- Adidas

Just do it.

- Nike

Think different.

- Apple

Play on words

Here, common phrases are manipulated and words with double meanings are used to appeal to the reader's intellect – making them feel clever for 'getting it':

Now arriving: fair fares.

- Air travel promotion

Great minds like a think.

- The Economist

Editerz Watned.

- Newspaper job post

Rhetorical question

Useful as an expansion after a short header, this questions the reader's position:

Can you afford not to switch?

- Electricity provider promotion

Are you ready for the future of television?

- TV channel package offer

Have you got what it takes?

- Gym class announcement

Numbers

This final strapline technique presents the reader with numeric information or data related to the performance of the product or the offer being advertised. Short bursts of enticing information which complement the header or the main image work well here:

30% off all oak furniture.

- *Home store promotion*

100's of chances to win.

- *Gambling advert*

Only £29.99 per square metre.

- *Flooring offer*

3. Wordplay and puns

Wordplay and puns serve as memory hooks that remain with the reader after they have encountered the advert. They also provide an opportunity for the creative manipulation of language.

Words inside words

This technique is best explained via demonstration, but basically involves placing key words within longer words:

*Com-**pet**-ition!*

- *Crufts poster*

Quest-*ion.*

- *Mystery adventure book promotion*

Secret-*ary.*

- *Thriller movie poster*

Homophones

Homophones are words which sound the same when pronounced, but have different meanings and are often spelled differently (e.g. 'new' and 'knew'). They can be substituted for one another to create phrases with double meanings:

Heaven Scent

- *Perfume promotion*

Rubber Banned.

- *Traffic notice*

Finnish First.

- *Racer biography advert*

Flour Power.

- *Cookbook poster*

Homographs

Homographs are words which are spelled the same but have different meanings and can be pronounced differently. Combining pairs of them in the same line, often as noun and verb, can give the phrase a clever double meaning:

Bank on our bank.

- *Financial institution advert*

Look cool, stay cool.

- *Beachwear promotion*

"It's not dear, dear!"

- *Banking advert*

Puns

This final wordplay technique exploits the different possible meanings of a word, or the fact that there are words which sound alike but have different meanings, often linking them to a well-known catchphrase:

Planet of the grapes.

- *Wine bar promotion*

Pizza my heart.

- *Italian restaurant advert*

Tiecoon.

- *Men's formalwear promotion*

Floors for thought.

- Flooring company advert

Sure Lock Homes.

- Home security promotion

4. Images

A broad range of images can be categorised in order to develop critical analysis of the visual features of persuasive adverts. These categories include:

A picture of the product

This type of image shows off the product so that the reader can see what is on offer. However, it also serves to present the product in its very best light, often embellishing and exaggerating quality. In reality, the reader may well find that the product is not quite what the image suggested (think of images of any popular fast food and compare it with the actual product served!).

A picture of the product in use

This image type demonstrates the enjoyment, efficiency or impact of the product and enables the reader to imagine themselves using it by mentally substituting themselves for the person in the image. The people in the advert are usually attractive, aspirational model-types, adding another layer of persuasion to the advert by making the reader aspire to be like them via attainment of the product.

Pictures of the 'results' of using the product

These could be real or hypothetical results. The focus here lies not on the product itself, but on what the product can **do**, and how it might **e**ffect a positive change in the reader's life, all the way from whiter teeth via the latest toothpaste, to a better quality of life for a child in a third world country through charitable sponsorship.

Metaphorical images

These are images that reinforce the message of the brand or the product, but are not actually related to either in any concrete way. For example, a sports equipment company might employ images that metaphorically represent **speed** in a visceral way, e.g. a cheetah or a fighter jet, even though there is no real comparison between these and the speeds of their sponsored athletes (or their customers).

Once examples of each of these image types have been found and analysed, pupils will again be more likely to employ a range of meaningful imagery in their persuasive adverts, and will also be more aware of the messages and purpose behind the images they see in advertising every day.

Structural model part 2: Persuasion

Having gained the reader's attention via the **engagement** techniques, the following persuasive methods encourage them to **act**. The key point to remember here (and the biggest difference between a persuasive advert and a persuasive essay or handout) is the need for brevity and economy of language. When selecting and combining the following techniques, the mantra must be 'to-the-point', and only the most effective phrases and vocabulary should be included.

5. Product claims

The following selection of persuasive techniques enable pupils to convey the advantages and/or results of using the advertised product. As referenced in the explanations for pictures of the product in use or its results, these 'results' may be exaggerated, embellished, overestimated and inflated. This should be discussed with pupils.

Certainty openers

These open with words that suggest a sure-fire result, leaving no room for uncertainty in the reader's mind:

Guaranteed to aid weight loss.

- Dietary product advert

Proven *to protect your fence for 10 years.*

- Fence coating promotion

Unquestionable *quality, every time.*

- Car servicing advert

Numbers

Including numerical data and statistics as 'proof' of the effectiveness of a product is a popular persuasive method. Remind pupils in their analysis of this technique to question the source - 'Where did the numerical data come from?' – You might even inform them that 87 per cent of statistics are invented!

9 out of 10 dentists use Pearl Paste at home.

- Toothpaste endorsement

Reduces visible wrinkles by 60%.

- Cosmetics promotion

Lasts twice as long as the named brand.

- Supermarket washing liquid promotion

Other numerical data, such as dates and periods of time, can also be employed persuasively:

Dries in less than 30 minutes!

- Kitchen appliance promotion

Established in 1890: over 100 years of experience.

- Family baker advert

3 in 1

Patterns of three have been used in powerful persuasive addresses for many years (e.g. 'Life, liberty, and the pursuit of happiness'; 'Friends, Romans, Countrymen'; 'Government of the people, by the people, for the people', etc.). The dramatic emphasis and persuasive energy they generate multiplies as the list builds:

Cleans, skins and chops in one easy action.

- Food blender advert

Goes, turns and stops like a real F1 racer.

- Remote control car promotion

Pause, rewind and record live TV.

- Digital TV advert

Change

Use of the key word 'change' reinforces the suggestion that acting on the message of the persuasive advert will effect a positive difference in the reader's life:

Our CleanQuick technology will change the way you wash clothes forever.

- Detergent advert

Our diet subs will help change your life for the better.

- Sandwich shop promotion

Your generosity could change the world for a child in need.

- Charity appeal

Once this technique is grasped, words other than 'change' may be used:

*Our CleanQuick technology will **revolutionise** the way you wash clothes.*

*Our diet subs will help **transform** your life for the better.*

*Your generosity could **save** the life of a child in need.*

No matter what

A variant of the 'certainty opener', this sentence type begins with the subordinate clause 'No matter what_____'. It implies that the subsequent results are guaranteed for **any** reader:

No matter what your age, you will love our Lemmington resort.

- Holiday resort promotion

No matter what your level of experience is, we can find the job for you.

- *Employment agency advert*

No matter what state your car is in, We Buy Your Car will take it!

- *Car buying service claim*

Endorsements

An endorsement is a public show of approval, usually by a respected professional or organisation. Including these in a persuasive advert may increase the reader's faith in the product, as they believe it has been tested and approved by a reliable person or group. Just remind pupils in their analysis of this technique that these 'reliable' agents may have been paid quite handsomely for their endorsement, and as such are unlikely to say anything negative about the product:

Recommended by What? Magazine.

- *Buyer guide endorsement*

Regulated and controlled by the Financial Board.

- *Loan company endorsement*

Winner of Good House Care's 'Product of the Year'.

- *Domestic appliance advert*

6. Offers

The inclusion of offers, such as price discounts and bulk buys, make the advertised product appear to be better value for money. Consequently, the reader feels positive about getting a 'good deal', and is thus more likely to part with their money. However, when analysing this technique it is useful to discuss how much the company advertising the product is really 'giving away'. You might introduce ideas like profit margins and marketing strategies during this discussion. Ask pupils, 'Why do these companies give offers? Do they like giving away money? Are they just that generous?' 'What is *really* going on?'

Now

The use of the word 'now' implies urgency, motivating the reader to act quickly:

Call now and get a free clock radio!

- Life insurance advert

Register now to get 20% off your first rental.

- Online movie rental promotion

Apply now, offer ends 18th February.

- Furniture finance promotion

BOGOF

BOGOF stands for 'buy one, get one free'. Discounts for multiple purchases can be worded in a range of ways:

Buy one, get one free!

- Double glazing promotion

Four coconuts for the price of two!

- Fruit promotion

Pay for 10 months and receive membership for the whole year.

- Golf club membership offer

Buy now, pay _____

This type of offer combines both implied urgency and deferred payment. It works by offering the reader the gratification of ownership now, without the immediate responsibility of paying for it.

Buy now, pay next year!

- Home improvement promotion

Buy now, pay over four years with 0% interest free credit!

- Jewellery finance advert

Borrow money now, pay when you are ready!

- Loan promotion

Percentage / fraction reduction

This simply informs the reader how much they will save compared with the original price (the obvious question for discussion being – 'Was the product ever worth the original price?'):

Get 25% off when you mention this advert.

- Restaurant deal

Half price with this coupon!

- Homeware store offer

All items 50% off in our end of season sale.

- Retail advert

Free! (But not really)

Introductory offers which include 'something for nothing' are an effective way of persuading a reader to commit to act:

£20 free bet when you sign up to BetFace.com.

- Online gambling offer

First month free trial with Webmovies.

- Online streaming movie service

Try a free sample of Chompbox today!

- Food delivery promotion

Tryout

Working in a similar way to the previous method, a free trial of a product or service is offered. A discussion about the strings that are attached to seemingly 'no-risk' or 'free' offers may be productive!

Book a test drive at your local dealership.

- Car promotion

Call in today for a free sample.

- Cosmetics advert

Try the pressure cleaner for a week with no obligation to buy!

- DIY promotion

When analysing these types of offers, pupils might be challenged to generate a 'what they really mean' extension:

Book a test drive at your local dealership – "Where a pushy salesperson will pressure you into buying."

Call in today for a free sample – "So we can bombard you with other offers and make you buy something."

7. Calls to action

These usually include imperative verbs, and function as a direct instruction to the reader to act. They create a sense of urgency and need, and work to convince the reader that they might miss out on a 'good thing' if they don't respond immediately.

Now

Introduced in method 6 (see page 190), this technique works well with both 'offers' and 'calls to action' by implying urgency through use of the key word 'now'. It is especially effective when combined with imperative verbs:

Join now at www.gymfittrain.com.

- Gym promotion

Act now, before it's too late for change!

- Animal conservation appeal

Book your tickets now!

- Holiday advert

If, then

This technique works by directly addressing the reader and suggesting a situation which may be current for them (perhaps one they may be unhappy with) starting with the word 'If'. It then goes on to suggest an alternative action they can take, beginning with 'then':

If you are thinking of starting a pension plan, then talk to us.

- Financial services advert

If you are tired of poor service and expensive bills, then give TB Broadband a try.

- Internet provider promotion

If you want to make a difference, then call Wildcare today.

- Animal conservation advert

Action first

This technique positions the imperative verb at the start of the sentence, followed by a succinct summary of the desired action.

Put yourself first.

- Financial planning advert

Sign up today.

- Donor appeal

Stop wasting time.

- Business solutions advert

Change

This technique works well with both 'product claims' and 'calls to action' by hinting at the (hypothetical) positive effect that attainment of the advertised product will have on the reader. This is achieved through the use of the key word 'change' (often used as an imperative verb):

Change your life, start saving today.

- Banking promotion

Make a change today, choose Healthsport Gym.

- *Gym membership advert*

Change your provider and save £££s

- *Internet provider advert*

Step-by-step

This technique is often included in adverts found in magazines or newspapers, where readers have more time to assimilate the information provided. They are comprised of a set of instructions (usually in patterns of 3, see page 188) and work to provide the reader with an easy, clear plan to follow; something they can act upon straight away:

Step 1: Register at www.boxybingo.com
Step 2: Deposit £10.
Step 3: Receive your £20 free bet and START PLAYING!

- *Online gambling promotion*

Step 1: Take a selfie while wearing your X-Star cap.
Step 2: Tweet it to @xstar with the hashtag #myxcap.
Step 3: Wait until July 7th for the big prize draw!

- *Clothing brand competition*

Step 1: Fill in and cut out the coupon below.
Step 2: Take it to your local Quickshop store.
Step 3: Trade it for your own copy of 'The Ace of Spades'.

- *Free book promotion*

Forms

A feature that often appears in adverts placed in magazines, newspapers, and especially in online promotions, this is a call to action that can have consequences far beyond the advert on the page. Forms are usually made up of prompts for information and space for the reader to input their responses:

Name: . . . .
Address line 1: . . . .

Address line 2: ....

Town: ....

County: ....

Postcode: ....

Date of birth: ....

Gender: ....

E-mail address: ....

Phone number: ....

The idea is that giving away all this personal information will lead to some sort of reward (price discount, entry into a prize draw etc.) Yet in reality it is more likely to result, at best, in plenty of spam mail coming through the door! While useful to include in an appropriate persuasive advert for pupils, this technique is perhaps even more useful as a way of discussing both data protection and identity theft.

Structural model part 3: Information

This final element supports the previous two in two main ways: by providing the reader with what they **need** to know, and by providing them with what they **have** to know. The difference is subtle, but while the aim of the first provision is to further aid the persuasive efforts of the advert, the aim of the second is to avoid getting the company into trouble for misleading the reader. Throughout this chapter we have looked at the manipulative methods advertisers use to persuade audiences, and we have seen how subtle they can be, how they can play fast and loose with the truth and exaggerate the claims and quality of what they are offering. However, by law, advertisers cannot **lie**, so within the 'information' element they are obliged to present the **truth**, often referred to as the 'fine print'. Once again, analysis of this element, along with the other types of information presented in this section, will not only provide pupils with useful writing tools which add authenticity to their work, but it will also draw their attention to the importance of the 'fine print', and help them to avoid falling for any unscrupulous persuasive methods.

8. Dates, times and product information

These techniques come under the umbrella of what the reader **needs** to know in order to act. They are quick, clear bursts of information and leave the reader in no doubt as to what to do next, and **when** they should do it.

Opening times

These are useful to include for places that a reader would have to physically visit, but can also be applied to events and special releases:

Open 9 a.m. to 8 p.m. Monday - Saturday.

- Retail information

Ticket hotline opens 9.00 a.m. on Saturday 7th July.

- Concert ticket sales line

Early opening for first day of sale — 5.00 a.m. in stores nationwide.

- Retail sale information

Event dates

These can be included in a variety of adverts for events that readers would either have to physically attend or complete an action by:

Lancaster Festival Weekend — Friday 6th — Sunday 9th June, 2015.

- Concert information

Online flash sale — one day only! Friday 4th July.

- Electronic sale event

Competition deadline — 5.00 p.m. on Monday 8th September.

- Phone-in competition

Sundays at 8 p.m.

- Television programme broadcast time

Time criticals

Time criticals reinforce a sense of urgency which will usually be evident in the rest of the advert:

Offer expires on Monday 18th May.

- Retail offer condition

Only available until 12th March.

- Electronic game sale event

Pre-order on 8th June, don't miss out!

- Film release advert

Supportive times

This final, time-based method serves to further persuade the reader by offering a service or guarantee which continues beyond the time of the initial purchase:

12-month unlimited warranty.

- Jewellery purchase information

24-hour technical support.

- Mobile phone contract offer

30-day money back guarantee.

- Home entertainment advert

9. Fine print

This is the section of the advert where advertisers place the information that the reader **has** to know, mainly so the company does not break the law for misleading their customers. It is usually confined to a small space at the bottom of a page, written in a diminutive point size (hence the names 'fine print,' and 'small print') where it often remains unread. Comparing and contrasting both the body and fine print of a single advert can prove both useful and/or alarming!

Time criticals

Placed in the small print, this technique can be used to limit the time an offer is available without making it overtly clear to the reader, to whom time pressures or constraints might be off-putting:

Offer expires 19.07.2014.

- Supermarket promotion

Only available between Monday and Thursday.

- Takeout two-for-one offer

Appointments on Mondays and Wednesdays only.

- Beauty retreat promotion

Legal phrases

These are often included in the fine print as a safeguard for the company against legal action from customers who feel they have been misled. Look out for the super-speed verbal examples at the end of radio adverts and compare the intonation of the delivery to the rest of the ad!

Subject to availability.

- Clothing shop promotion

Selected stores only.

- Home furniture offer

No purchase necessary.

- Cereal giveaway promotion

Your statutory rights are not affected.

- Department store offer

Votes made after lines close will not be counted but may still be charged.

- Phone-in competition rule

The 'real' numbers

These are the 'numbers behind the numbers'. They add clarity and often give a much better insight into how the statistics were generated:

75% of the 93 women polled agreed that they saw a difference after using our product.

- Cosmetics promotion

Items in the sale have been sold at the original price in at least 50% of our stores, within the last 100 days.

- Retail sale offers

70% of users reported positive results after 6 months of using the product.

- Cosmetics promotion

Trademarks

These establish intellectual property ownership, patents and copyright for companies. By using them, pupils will add an air of authenticity to their persuasive adverts:

All rights reserved.

- Sports equipment advert

Copyright ArtStar Records, 2014.

- Music promotion

Buzzstar is a registered trademark of Buzzstar Drinks Ltd.

- Energy drink advert

Health warnings

This is another technique used by companies to avoid getting into trouble if their product ends up producing undesired effects for a user:

Not recommended for pregnant women, people over 75, or people with a heart condition.

- Energy drink promotion

Not intended for prolonged use.

- Exercise supplement advert

Consult a doctor if irritation occurs.

- Cosmetics promotion

10. Web links and social media

Unlike small print, this final element is likely to be displayed visibly in a prominent position within the text. The reason for this is that social media has become a key marketing tool for many companies. It allows them to target their audience quickly, tailor content, move rapidly with any advances in products or trends and all for a relatively low outlay (especially when compared to outlets such as magazine print and television advertising). One difficult challenge you could set the pupils is to ask them to find an advert that does **not** have an internet link of some kind – they will be hard-pressed to do so, and it will bring home the importance of its inclusion in their own persuasive adverts. It will also enable you to start a conversation about e-safety and protecting yourself online.

Electronic links

Often these assume the form of URLs or QR codes:

www.rockenergydrinks.com

- *Energy drink website*

www.youtube.com/tornadofc

- *Football team YouTube channel*

www.beautyfirst.blogspot.net

- *Cosmetics blog*

Contact

This final technique provides the reader with a way of contacting the company, interacting with them and spreading the company's message to the reader's friends - essentially making them an advertising agent!

www.facebook.com/iconzclothing

- *Clothing Facebook page*

www.twitter.com/animaid

- *Animal aid twitter page*

contact@greenpowerparty.gov.uk

- *Political e-mail contact*

PREPARE YOURSELF...

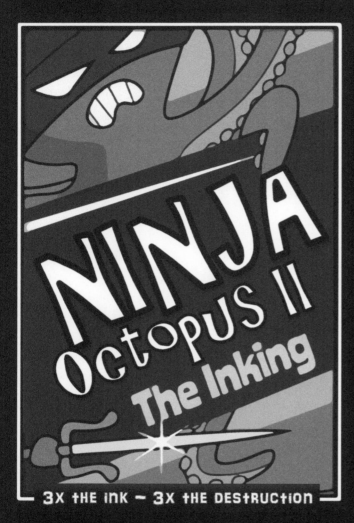

3X THE INK – 3X THE DESTRUCTION

ARE YOU READY TO TAKE ON AN ARMY OF MUTANT SQUIRRELS, LED BY THE MURDEROUS MERCENARY, SERGEANT SLAUGHTERGUTS?

PLAY THROUGH TEN GUT-BUSTING LEVELS OF OCTOPUS-ON-SQUIRREL WARFARE.

SLICE, DICE AND INK YOUR WAY TO A FACE-TO-SUCKER SHOWDOWN WITH YOUR RE-ANIMATED MUTANT ENEMY.

"EVEN MORE SQUIRREL CARNAGE THAN THE FIRST GAME – I COULD BARELY KEEP MY EYES OPEN, AND MY LUNCH DOWN!"
– MAX HARDCASTLE – GAMEMAG.COM

DOWNLOAD THE FIRST LEVEL FOR

FREE
at WWW.NINJAVSSQUIRREL.COM

...INKY VENGEANCE IS COMING.

OUT 12TH APRIL
PRE-ORDER BEFORE THE 10TH APRIL AND RECEIVE EXCLUSIVE DLC,

INCLUDING LIMITED EDITION 'ROBOT NINJA' ARMOUR.

TWEET SCREENSHOTS at @NINJAVSSQUIRREL

OUT NOW!

WWW.THECEPRESS.COM

★★★★★
"5 OUT OF 5"
"A MUST-HAVE BOOK FOR THE KS2 CLASSROOM!"
SETH FELTON – Y6 TEACHER

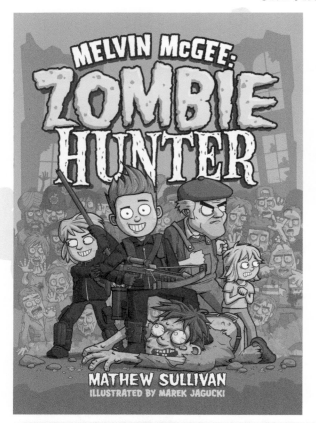

EVER HAD ONE OF THOSE DAYS WHERE EVERYTHING SEEMS TO GO WRONG?

YOUR TOWN GETS INVADED BY AN ARMY OF BRAIN-SCOFFING ZOMBIES, YOU GET TRAPPED INSIDE AN ARMOURED SUPERMARKET, AND YOU ARE LUMPED WITH THE RESPONSIBILITY OF SAVING THE WORLD... ALL ON YOUR BIRTHDAY!

HAVE YOU EVER HAD ONE OF THOSE DAYS?

YOU HAVEN'T?

WELL, MELVIN MCGEE IS HAVING ONE OF THOSE DAYS...

...AND IT'S NOT EVEN LUNCH TIME YET.

@Reece * 🔵 Follow

I love the way you have made a trailer from the blurb. I think Melvin and his family are fantastic!

@Ella * 🔵 Follow

I think your book is super! My favourite character so far is Melvin! Love the birthday scene! #getoutofbed!

@Thomas * 🔵 Follow

Zombie Hunter! Need this book so bad! Watched the trailer - awesome! Cannot wait to get my hands on this. #checkitout

@Katie * 🔵 Follow

What a trailer! I thoroughly enjoyed the first two chapters of your book and can't wait to read more! #hilarious

* Actual comments from pupils at St Paschal Baylon Primary School

FOR ALL ALAN PEAT LTD TRAINING, INSET AND
CONFERENCE DETAILS GO TO

www.alanpeat.com

Follow Alan on

@alanpeat

fb.com/alanpeatltdapps